The Forbidden Schoolhouse

The True and Dramatic Story of Prudence Crandall and Her Students

Suzanne Jurmain

Houghton Mifflin Company ~ Boston 2005

www.houghtonmifflinbooks.com

The text of this book is set in Perpetua.
Photo credits can be found on page 150.

Back jacket quote: From letter to the *Windham County Advertiser,* May 7, 1833,
reprinted in the *Liberator*, May 25, 1833.

Library of Congress Cataloging-in-Publication Data

Jurmain, Suzanne.
The forbidden schoolhouse : the true and dramatic story of Prudence Crandall and her students/ by Suzanne Tripp Jurmain.
p. cm.
Includes bibliographical references.
ISBN 0-618-47302-5 (hardcover)
1. Crandall, Prudence, 1803–1890—Juvenile literature. 2. Women educators—Connecticut—Biography—Juvenile literature.
3. African American women—Education—Connecticut—History—Juvenile literature. I. Title.
LA2317.C73J87 2005
370'.92—dc22

2004026554

ISBN-13: 978-0618-47302-1

Printed in China
SCP 10 9 8 7 6 5 4

For Beth—another fighter

Contents

Acknowledgments

NOBODY WRITES A BOOK ALONE, and many, many people have helped make this one a reality.

My thanks go first to my agents Christina Biamonte, Tracey Adams, and Edward Necarsulmer at McIntosh and Otis and to my editor, Ann Rider, whose enthusiasm and incisive comments have helped me over many rough patches.

To my brother David Tripp, photographer, writer, and confidant extraordinaire, I owe a huge debt. Not only did he and his wife, Susan, feed and house me during a research trip to the East Coast, but David drove through a snowstorm so that I could visit Prudence Crandall's house and risked frostbite in order to take many of the lovely photos that grace this volume.

I am also deeply grateful to Kazimiera Kozlowski, curator of the Prudence Crandall Museum in Canterbury,

Connecticut, who patiently answered my queries, supplied photos, and spent a day showing me through Prudence's house.

Teresa Coble, a wonderful researcher at the Kansas State Historical Society, combed the archives, sent me reams of material, and was always ready to listen to my requests for more documents. At the New-York Historical Society Mariam Touba uncovered obscure reference material. Jeannine Sherman at the Connecticut State Library kindly tracked down and sent me additional information, and Jeff Bridgers at the Library of Congress helped to unearth some wonderful photographic material. My thanks also go to Lawrence Stack of Stack's Rare Coins in New York City for generously allowing me to reproduce photos from one of their catalogues and to Mr. Stack's assistant, Vicken Yegparian, for having those images copied and sent so expeditiously.

Last, but most definitely not least, my greatest thanks go to my husband, Richard, who makes all things possible.

A Note to the Reader

It is important to remember that many of the words used to refer to race in earlier times are not words we would use today. In Prudence Crandall's day, for example, it was considered polite to refer to African Americans as "colored people" or "Negroes." Then, as now, the word "nigger" was often used as an insult. Because these are the terms Prudence, her friends, and her enemies actually used, they appear in many quotations in this book. The original words have been used for the sake of accuracy and to show how people who lived more than 170 years ago actually spoke and thought.

Chapter I

"A Little More Learning"

NO ONE COULD LOOK at Prudence Crandall without noticing the intelligence in her steady blue eyes. In fact, there was no question about it. Prudence was smart. Very smart. She'd graduated from one of the finest boarding schools in New England. For several years she'd taught children at two village schools in Connecticut. Now, at age twenty-eight—at a time when most young women were married and taking care of families—Prudence had bought a large house with plenty of space for classrooms and opened her very own school right in the middle of the little town of Canterbury, Connecticut.

It was no ordinary school, either. The Canterbury Female

Prudence Crandall's schoolhouse in Canterbury today. The big house had plenty of space for classrooms and boarders.

Boarding School, officially opened in October 1831, already ranked as one of the best private girls' academies in the state. The pupils came from wealthy, important local families. Some of the most prominent men in Canterbury were members of its board of visitors, and the school's reputation was so good that girls from distant towns were coming to live at the schoolhouse as boarders.

If Prudence looked out her classroom window on a sunny afternoon, she could see the girls in their long skirts and bonnets chattering as they walked in the garden or sat under the big chestnut tree doing their lessons. And they had plenty of lessons. Although many nineteenth-century people thought educating women was a waste, Prudence didn't agree. She expected her girls to learn. Reading, writing, math, geography, history, philosophy, chemistry, and astronomy were part of the school's curriculum. Some pupils also took classes in painting, piano, and French. On Sundays all students were expected to go to church.

The girls were cheerful. The school was busy. Even the Connecticut countryside around Canterbury looked like a pretty landscape painting. There were orchards, shady trees, and small, prosperous farms nestled among the rolling hills. But out beyond those peaceful farms and meadows, a terrible

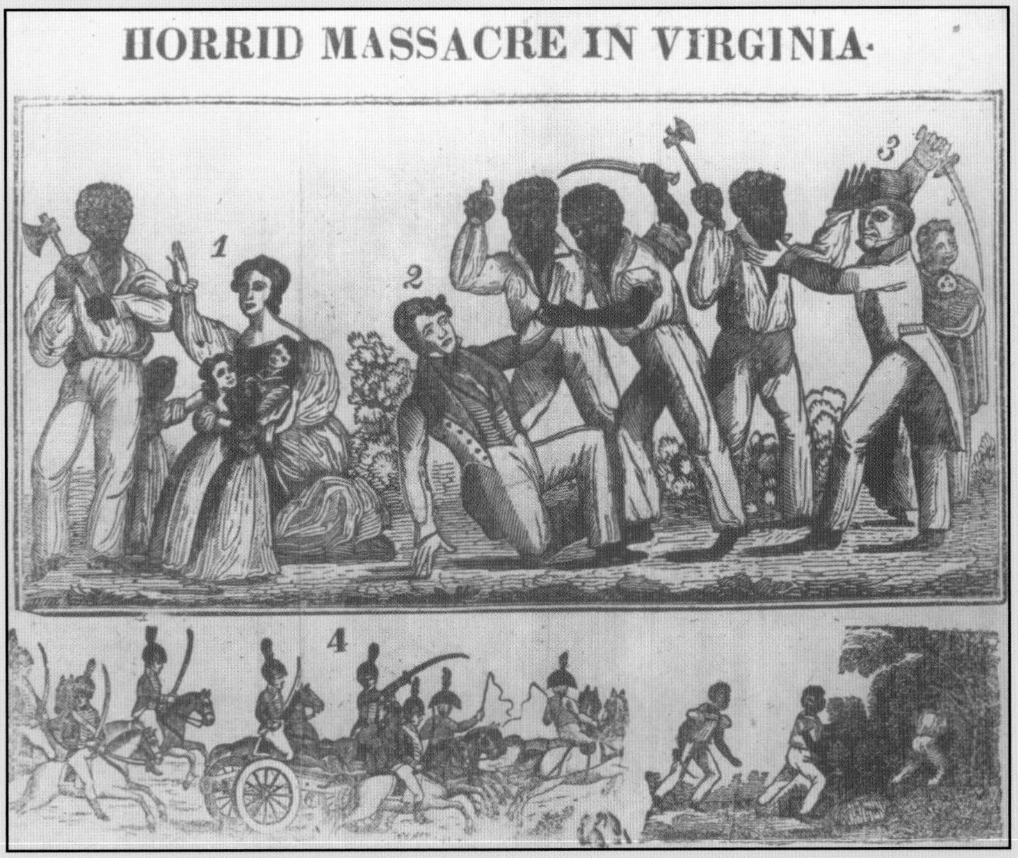

Print showing the bloody slave rebellion led by Nat Turner. This revolt, which occurred in the same year Prudence opened her school, fueled antiblack feeling and made it harder for opponents of slavery to arouse sympathy for African Americans.

THE LIBERATOR.

OL. I. WILLIAM LLOYD GARRISON AND ISAAC KNAPP, PUBLISHERS. No. 1

BOSTON, MASSACHUSETTS.] OUR COUNTRY IS THE WORLD—OUR COUNTRYMEN ARE MANKIND. [SATURDAY, JANUARY 1, 1831.

HE LIBERATOR
IS PUBLISHED WEEKLY
AT NO. 6, MERCHANTS' HALL.

WM. L. GARRISON, EDITOR.

Stephen Foster, Printer.

TERMS.

☞ Two Dollars per annum, payable in ance.
☞ Agents allowed every sixth copy, gra-
☞ No subscription will be received for a rter period than six months.
☞ All letters and communications must POST PAID.

THE LIBERATOR.

THE SALUTATION.

date my being from the opening year,
me, a stranger in this busy sphere,
ere some I meet perchance may pause and ask,
at is my name, my purpose, or my task!

name is 'LIBERATOR'! I propose
hurl my shafts at freedom's deadliest foes!
task is hard—for I am charged to save
n from his brother!—to redeem the slave!

who may hear, and yet condemn my cause,
, shall the best of Nature's holy laws
trodden down? and shall her open veins
w but for cement to her offspring's chains?

thou a parent? shall thy children be
t from thy breast, like branches from the tree,
I doom'd to servitude, in helplessness,
other shores, and thou ask no redress?

ou, in whose bosom glows the sacred flame
filial love, say, if the tyrant came,
force thy parent shrieking from thy sight,
ould thy heart bleed—*because thy face is white?*

thou a brother? shall thy sister twine
r feeble arm in agony on thine,
d thou not lift the heel, nor aim the blow
him who bears her off to life-long wo?

thou a sister? will no desp'rate cry
ake thy sleeping brother, while thine eye
holds the fetters locking on the limb
etched out in rest, which hence, must end, for him?

thou a lover?—no! nought e'er was found
lover's breast, save cords of love, that bound
n to his kind! then, thy profession save!
rswear affection or release thy slave!

ou who art kneeling at thy Maker's shrine,
k if Heaven takes such offerings as thine!
n thy bonds the son of Afric sighs,
r higher than thy prayer his groans will rise!

d is a God of mercy, and would see
e prison doors unbarr'd—the bondmen free!
is a God of truth, with purer eyes
an to behold the oppressor's sacrifice!

arice, thy cry and thine insatiable thirst
ke man consent to see his brother cursed!
ars, sweat and blood thou drink'st, but, in their

less, prejudice more stubborn, and apathy more frozen than among slave owners themselves. Of course there were individual exceptions to the contrary. This state of things afflicted, but did not dishearten me. I determined, at every hazard, to lift up the standard of emancipation in the eyes of the nation, *within sight of Bunker Hill and in the birth place of liberty.* That standard is now unfurled; and long may it float, unhurt by the spoliations of time or the missiles of a desperate foe—yea, till every chain be broken, and every bondman set free. Let southern oppressors tremble—let their secret abettors tremble—let their northern apologists tremble—let all the enemies of the persecuted blacks tremble.

I deem the publication of my original Prospectus* unnecessary, as it has obtained a wide circulation. The principles therein inculcated will be steadily pursued in this paper, excepting that I shall not array myself as the political partisan of any man. In defending the great cause of human rights, I wish to derive the assistance of all religions and of all parties.

Assenting to the 'self-evident truth' maintained in the American Declaration of Independence, 'that all men are created equal, and endowed by their Creator with certain inalienable rights—among which are life, liberty, and the pursuit of happiness,' I shall strenuously contend for the immediate enfranchisement of our slave population. In Park-street Church, on the Fourth of July, 1829, in an address on slavery, I unreflectingly assented to the popular but pernicious doctrine of *gradual* abolition. I seize this opportunity to make a full and unequivocal recantation, and thus publicly to ask pardon of my God, of my country, and of my brethren the poor slaves, for having uttered a sentiment so full of timidity, injustice, and absurdity. A similar recantation from my pen was published in the Genius of Universal Emancipation at Baltimore, in September, 1829. My conscience is now satisfied.

I am aware, that many object to the severity of my language; but is there not cause for severity? I *will be* as harsh as truth, and as uncompromising as justice. On this subject I do not wish to think, or speak, or write, with moderation. No! no! Tell a man whose house is on fire, to give a moderate alarm; tell him to moderately rescue his wife from the hands of the ravisher; tell the mother to gradually extricate her babe from the fire into which it has fallen;—but urge me not to use moderation in a cause like the present. I am in earnest—I will not equivocate—I will not excuse—I will not retreat a single inch—AND I WILL BE HEARD.

DISTRICT OF COLUMBIA.

What do many of the professed enemies of slavery mean, by heaping all their reproaches upon the South, and asserting that the crime of oppression is not national? What power but Congress—and Congress by the authority of the American people—has jurisdiction over the District of Columbia? That District is rotten with the plague, and stinks in the nostrils of the world. Though it is the Seat of our National Government,—open to the daily inspection of foreign ambassadors,—and ostensibly opulent with the congregated wisdom, virtue and intelligence of the land,—yet a fouler spot scarcely exists on earth. In it the worst features of slavery are exhibited; and as a mart for slave-traders, it is unequalled. These facts are well known to our two or three hundred representatives, but no remedy is proposed; they are known, if not minutely at least generally, to our whole population,—but who calls for redress?

Hitherto, a few straggling petitions, relative to this subject, have gone into Congress; but they have been too few to denote much public anxiety, or to command a deferential notice. It is certainly time that a vigorous and systematic effort should be made, from one end of the country to the other, to pull down that national monument of oppression which towers up in the District. We do hope that the 'earthquake voice' of the people will this session shake the black fabric to its foundation.

The following petition is now circulating in this city, and has obtained several valuable signatures. A copy may be found at the bookstore of LINCOLN & EDMANDS, No. 59 Washington-st., for a few days longer, where all the friends of the cause are earnestly invited to go and subscribe.

Petition to Congress for the Abolition of Slavery in the District of Columbia.

To the Honorable Senate and House of Representatives of the United States of America in Congress assembled, the petition of the undersigned citizens of Boston in Massachusetts and its vicinity respectfully represents—

That your petitioners are deeply impressed with the evils arising from the existence of slavery in the District of Columbia. While our Declaration of Independence boldly proclaims as self-evident truths, 'that all men are created equal, that they are endowed by their Creator with certain inalienable rights, that among these are life, liberty, and the pursuit of happiness,'—at the very seat of government human beings are born, almost daily, whom the laws pronounce to be from their birth, not *equal* to other men, and who are, for life, deprived of *liberty* and the *free pursuit of happiness.* The inconsistency of the conduct of our nation with its political creed, has brought

[From the Washington Spectator of Dec. 4.]

THE SLAVE TRADE IN THE CAPITAL

'The tender ties of husband, father, friend,
All bonds of nature in that moment end,
And each endures, while yet he draws his breat
A stroke as fatal as the scythe of death;
They lose in tears, the far receding shore,
But not the thought that they must meet no mo

It is well, perhaps, the American peo should know, that while we reiterate our bo of liberty in the ears of nations, and send b across the Atlantic our shouts of joy at triumph of liberty in France, we ourselves busily engaged in the work of oppressi Yes, let it be known to the citizens of Ameri that at the very time when the process which contained the President of the Uni States and his Cabinet was marching in umph to the Capitol, to celebrate the victo of the French over their oppressors, anot kind of procession was marching another w and that consisted of colored human bein handcuffed in pairs, and driven along by w had the appearance of a man on a horse! similar scene was repeated on Saturday la a *drove* consisting of males and females ch ed in couples, starting from Roby's tavern foot, for Alexandria, where with others, t are to embark on board a slave-ship in w ing to convey them to the South. While are writing, a colored man enters our roo and begs us to inform him if we can point any person who will redeem his friend immured in Alexandria jail, in a state of d tress amounting almost to distraction.* has been a faithful servant of a revolution officer who recently died—has been sol auction—parted from affectionate parent and from decent and mourning friends. own servant, with others, of whom we speak in commendatory terms, went down Alexandria to bid him farewell, but they w refused admittance to his cell, as was s 'the sight of his friends made him so.' He bears the reputation of a pi man. It is but a few weeks since we a ship with her cargo of slaves in the por Norfolk, Va.; on passing up the river, another ship off Alexandria, swarming w the victims of human cupidity. Such the scenes enacting in the heart of American nation. Oh, patriotism! wh is thy indignation! Oh, philanthropy! wh is thy grief? Oh, SHAME, WHERE IS T BLUSH! Well may the generous and no minded O'Connell say of the American c zen, '*I tell him he is a hypocrite. Look at stain in your star-spangled standard that never struck down in battle. I turn from Declaration of American Independence, an tell him that he has declared to God and ma lie, and before God and man I arraign him a hypocrite.*' Yes, thou soul of fire, glori O'Connell, if thou could but witness spectacles in Washington that make the ge of liberty droop her head in shame, and w her tears away in deep silence and undiss bled sorrow, you would lift your voice to to of thunder, but you would make your heard. Where is the O'Connell of this public that will plead for the EMANCIPAT OF THE DISTRICT OF COLUMBIA! Th shocking scenes must cease from amongst

The first page of the first edition of the *Liberator,* published January 1, 1831. In it William Lloyd Garrison promised to be "harsh as truth, and as uncompromising as justice" in the battle against slavery. "I will not excuse," he wrote, "I will not retreat a single inch—AND I WILL BE HEARD."

storm was brewing. In 1831 a great national battle over slavery was beginning, and Americans were taking sides.

In the South, a black preacher named Nat Turner organized a small band of slaves into an army and attacked white Virginians. By the time Turner and his followers were captured, they had brutally murdered fifty-five white men, women, and children.

In the North, a small number of people called abolitionists demanded that the U.S. government ban (or abolish) slavery and free all slaves *immediately*.

In Washington, D.C., the U.S. Congress ignored the requests of thousands of Americans and refused to end slavery in the nation's capital.

In Boston, William Lloyd Garrison, a twenty-six-year-old white man, published the first issues of a fiery antislavery newspaper called the *Liberator*.

And in Tarboro, North Carolina, the editor of the *North Carolina Free Press* told readers that the *Liberator* was downright dangerous. People who wanted to end slavery ought to be "barbecued," he said.

Prudence wasn't an abolitionist, but she sympathized with slaves. She'd been raised as a Quaker, and, like all Quakers, she'd been taught that slavery was a sin. Still, the quarrel over slavery didn't seem to have much to do with her. She didn't live in the South. She wasn't a slave owner. In 1831 it was still legal to own a slave in Connecticut, but almost no one did. Most of the blacks in Connecticut were free. In fact, there were so few African Americans in the state that people in some remote places had never seen a dark-skinned person. That wasn't true in Canterbury. About sixty-nine black people lived near the town. One, a young girl named Mariah, actually helped with the housekeeping at Prudence's school.

Mariah read the *Liberator*. Since the paper looked interesting, Prudence borrowed a copy and then sat down to read.

Slowly her eyes traveled down the printed pages, past hair-raising stories about slaves who'd been beaten, about slaves who'd made miraculous escapes, about slave families that had been torn apart when parents and children were sold to different owners—and that was only the beginning. Garrison's paper damned southerners who believed that slavery had been invented by God. It lashed out at northerners who refused to give free blacks decent jobs or decent educations. It attacked people who thought blacks didn't belong in America and should be sent back to Africa—and every word in the *Liberator* went straight to Prudence's heart.

Prudence wrote later that as she read the smudgy printed sheets, she felt her "feelings . . . awaken." She saw that "the prejudice of the whites against color was deep." For the first time in her life, as she explained in a newspaper article, Prudence began to wonder if she could do something—anything—that "might . . . serve the people of color."

It was a fine idea, but—aside from letting Mariah sit in on class sessions when the housekeeping chores were done—Prudence didn't make any immediate plans for helping blacks. Running the school took most of her energy. There were lessons to teach and papers to grade. She had to deal with parents and students and make sure that the school was clean, that the boarders were fed, and that the garden was cared for.

Sometimes as she rushed through the days, Prudence noticed that another African-American girl stopped by to visit Mariah. Still, that didn't seem important—until one September day in 1832 when Mariah's friend, Sarah Harris, asked to speak to Prudence.

"Miss Crandall," Sarah said, "I want to get a little more learning, enough . . . to teach colored children. If you will admit me to your school," she went on, "I shall forever be under the greatest obligation to you."

Prudence looked at the girl. Sarah was about nineteen or

twenty, and so fair-skinned she looked almost white. She belonged to the local church. Her father, who lived a few miles down the road, was a prosperous, respectable farmer.

Carefully, Sarah explained that she did not want to be a boarder. She'd be happy to walk to school from her father's farm each day. The only thing she really wanted was a chance to study. Of course, she knew it was a big request. Some parents and students might object to having a black pupil in the classes. If Prudence had to refuse because of that, Sarah said, she understood. She didn't want to be "the means of injuring" Prudence or the school.

Sarah Harris Fayerweather, Prudence's first black student, as an old woman.

Sarah sounded sincere, but her request was extraordinary. Prudence couldn't make a snap decision. Gently, she told Sarah she would have to think about it.

And there was a lot of thinking to do.

Prudence wanted to help black people. She believed education was important. She wanted to teach women. There were lots of good emotional reasons to say yes to Sarah.

There were also a lot of sensible reasons to say no.

First, admitting a black student was almost certain to cause an uproar. Although free blacks lived in the North, they weren't welcome. In most northern states African Americans could not vote, sit on juries, or run for office. White businessmen often refused to hire blacks. White laborers were sometimes unwilling to work alongside African Americans, and blacks were usually forced to sit apart from whites in churches and on stagecoaches. To many northerners, African Americans were no better than animals or criminals; and a visiting British college professor was shocked to find that some white Americans viewed the free blacks who lived in northern cities as "a curse and a contagion."

Prudence didn't believe that blacks and whites ought to be treated differently. But what if the parents of her white students did? What if white parents objected to having Sarah in class? What if they pulled their children out of her school? If too many students left, the school would be ruined. And what would Prudence do then? She had worked hard to establish her school. She needed the income to live. "No" was the sensible answer to Sarah's request.

But how could Prudence say it? How could she give up

everything she believed? How could she face the disappointment in Sarah's eyes?

For Prudence, there was only one answer.

In January 1833 a new student named Sarah Harris took her seat at one of the desks in Prudence's classroom.

Old-fashioned school desk now on display at the Prudence Crandall house. Desks like these may have been used by her pupils.

Chapter 2

"The School May Sink"

SUDDENLY, THE TOWN began to talk. Girls in the Crandall school told their mothers about Sarah. Wives told their husbands. Women chatted about it. Businessmen discussed it. Even farmers gossiped about it.

Have you heard? people probably said. There's a black girl in Miss Crandall's school.

A black *student?*

Yes, a black student sitting in the same classroom as the white girls!

It was big news. Shocking news. And the well-to-do parents of Prudence's white pupils were furious. It wasn't right, they objected. They didn't want their pampered daughters going to school with a "nigger girl." Why, just a few years ago in 1831, angry white citizens in nearby New Haven, Connecticut, had decided that it would be "destructive to the best interests of the city" if they allowed abolitionists to open a school for black men in their town. Some whites claimed that educating blacks would encourage bloody rebellions like Nat Turner's. Others said that letting blacks into schools would somehow lead to the mixing of the black and white races. Most school parents, however, seemed to agree on one point: Miss Crandall had to expel Sarah Harris.

Canterbury, Connecticut, as it looked in Prudence's day. Prudence's schoolhouse is at the far left.

A few told Prudence's father, who owned a farm near Canterbury, that they planned to take their girls out of his daughter's school immediately. Others were more direct.

Mrs. White, the wife of a local minister, told Prudence that the townsfolk did not want their children sitting in class with a black girl.

If Prudence did not expel Sarah, the woman added, white parents would remove their daughters and the school would "sink."

"The school may sink," Prudence snapped back, "but I will not give up Sarah Harris."

The words were brave. The threat was serious. Without students, the school *would* sink. Prudence might not be able to repay the money she'd borrowed to buy the school building. And, there was another problem. If the school ended with a scandal, would anyone ever hire her as a teacher again?

It was a bad situation. The parents were upset. The townspeople were disturbed. Even the school's honorary board of visitors—which was supposed to advise Prudence on plans and policy—had told her that admitting Sarah was a terrible mistake. But that wasn't surprising. The seven important Canterbury men who made up the board weren't particularly interested in helping African Americans. In fact, at least one member, Prudence's neighbor, Andrew T. Judson, belonged to the American Colonization Society. Like other Colonization Society members (including President Andrew Jackson), he was sure that whites were superior to blacks, and that God intended to keep the two races separate. Bringing blacks to America had been a terrible mistake, the Society said, because it had burdened the country with slavery, racial conflict, and a large number of poor free African Americans. The only way to solve those problems, Judson and his fellow Colonization Society members believed, was to send all black Americans—both free and slaves—back to Africa, as quickly as possible.

Mr. Judson would never approve of having Sarah in school. That was plain. It was also plain that others in Canterbury shared his views. Indeed, the only bright spot in the whole ugly mess was the students. The white girls at Prudence's school didn't seem a bit upset about having Sarah Harris as a classmate. Some of them had known Sarah for years. As young children they'd sat with her in classes at the local public elementary school. For some reason their parents hadn't been upset about that.

At the moment, however, one thing was clear. Things couldn't go on as they were. Prudence had to do something. Expelling Sarah was the easy solution, but Prudence never

Desk and chair displayed in the Prudence Crandall house today. Prudence may have sat at a desk that looked like this when she originally wrote to William Lloyd Garrison in 1833.

considered that. She had promised to give Sarah an education. She was determined to help black people. Besides, Prudence was stubborn. As a child, she'd been scolded for being disobedient. Her own brother said she was a "very obstinate girl." Prudence wouldn't go back on her word. She wasn't going to give in. But she did have a plan.

On January 18, 1833, Prudence sat down at her desk. She pulled out a clean sheet of paper, dipped her pen in the inkwell, and started to write a letter to Mr. William Lloyd Garrison, the abolitionist editor of the *Liberator.*

"Mr. Garrison," Prudence began, "I am to you, sir . . . an entire stranger." She introduced herself briefly. Then, as her pen scratched across the paper, she moved on to the main topic: Did the editor think she ought to close her present school for white girls and open a brand-new school—a school that would teach *only* young black women? Did Mr. Garrison think it was possible to find "20 or 25 young ladies of color" who would attend that new school and pay tuition and board of twenty-five dollars per quarter? In a few days, Prudence said, she would be in Boston to discuss the matter. In the meantime, would Mr. Garrison please keep her plan to open an academy for black girls secret? If her Canterbury neighbors found out, Prudence explained, "it would ruin . . . [her] present school."

Finally she signed it, "Yours, with greatest respect, Prudence Crandall."

Prudence sealed the letter. She put it in the mail, and waited to see what Mr. Garrison would say.

Chapter 3

"Six Scholars"

In the next few days, Prudence was busy. She told people in Canterbury that she had to make a trip to Boston—to visit schools and purchase teaching supplies, she said. Bundled in her winter woolens, with her bag in hand, she boarded the stagecoach and spent most of a day rattling along the country roads that led from Connecticut ninety miles north to Massachusetts.

In Boston she dismounted, registered at the Marlboro Hotel, and quickly penned a note:

January 29, 1833

Mr. Garrison: The lady that wrote you a short time since would inform you that she is now in town, and should be very thankful if you would call . . . and see her a few moments this evening at 6 o'clock.

As the day wore on, Prudence waited. She was a single woman, alone in a strange city. Beyond his name, his profession, and the fact that some people called him a "madman," she knew nothing about the man she was going to meet. She didn't even know what he looked like. Prudence wasn't a timid woman. Still, she must have been relieved when a slender, balding, scholarly-looking young man in wire spectacles politely introduced himself as William Lloyd Garrison.

Mr. Garrison must have been almost as relieved to see Prudence. Ever since he'd decided to work for the immediate abolition of slavery, Garrison had been fighting a hard, lonely battle. In the North and South people said he was a crazy "fanatic." He'd been fined and imprisoned for calling slave-

William Lloyd Garrison, editor of the *Liberator*, as he looked when Prudence met him.

trading sea captains "murderers" and "robbers." One southern legislature had offered a reward for his capture, dead or alive. And those were only some of Garrison's problems.

In 1833, many Americans still supported slavery. Many others hated both slavery and abolitionists. They thought slavery was evil but feared that giving immediate freedom to millions of poor, uneducated black slaves might hurt the U.S. economy, flood the country with beggars and criminals, and cause a serious break between the North and the South. So few white Americans supported the abolitionist cause that in 1831 only twenty-five of Garrison's five hundred subscribers to the *Liberator* were white. Things were so bad that sometimes, in low moments, Garrison must have felt that he was trying to change the world single-handedly. When a friend urged him to "keep more cool," the editor explained, "I . . . need to be *all on fire,* for I have mountains of ice . . . to melt."

To melt those mountains, Garrison needed allies, and Prudence was ready, willing, and able to help. Besides, she was a teacher.

That was particularly important.

If black people were ever going to win equal rights and good jobs in America, they needed education. Garrison and his supporters knew that. But African Americans found that learning was very hard to come by. So few U.S. schools and colleges were willing to teach black pupils that in 1865, when the Civil War ended, only one out of every twenty African Americans could read.

In the 1830s, southerners were so afraid that educated blacks might rebel against slavery that they passed laws against teaching African Americans. In South Carolina a white person who taught a black person to read could be sentenced to six months in prison and a hundred-dollar fine. If a free African American taught another black person to read, the punishment was fifty lashes and a fifty-dollar fine. The sentence for a slave who dared to teach his own child to read was fifty strokes of the whip.

In the North, where many feared that educated blacks might take jobs from white workers, black children were seldom allowed to enter white schools. White teachers rarely taught black pupils, and schools for African Americans were scarce. Philadelphia, the home of twenty thousand blacks, was typical. There were only three schools and four teachers for all the African-American children in the entire city.

Now, Prudence was planning to do something about this terrible problem. Not only was she planning to open a school for African-American girls, but she was offering to teach advanced grammar, math, and science—the sorts of subjects that would eventually allow her black students to teach other African-American pupils. It was like a dream come true. Garrison was enthusiastic. He wanted to help. As they sat together in the Marlboro Hotel that evening, he advised Prudence. He encouraged her. He also gave her the names of several black families whose daughters might come to her school.

One family lived in Providence, and Prudence immediately caught the stagecoach headed south to Rhode Island.

The address was in a seedy, rundown city neighborhood. A lot of middle-class white women wouldn't have gone near the place, but Prudence cautiously picked her way past the garbage, the shabby buildings, and the bars and entered a boardinghouse run by Mrs. Elizabeth Hammond.

It was worth the trip.

Mrs. Hammond, a widow, welcomed the schoolteacher with open arms. Thanks to a small inheritance and careful saving, she could afford to give her two daughters a good education. Mrs. Hammond immediately asked Prudence to sign up her girls, nine-year-old Sarah and seventeen-year-old Ann Eliza, as pupils. Then she introduced Prudence to three other black families who also wanted to educate their daughters.

To African Americans like these, school was not a burden or a chore. It was a gateway to a new, exciting world of knowledge. It was a means of showing that African Americans were just as smart as white people. Above all, it was, in the words of a group of black school planners, a road to "positions of responsibility and trust . . . distinction and happiness." Booker T. Washington, a former slave and founder of one of the first colleges for blacks, expressed the feelings of many when he said school was "the greatest place on earth." The families Prudence met in Rhode Island were hungry for learning, and Prudence was thrilled. "I think," she wrote to Garrison, "I shall be able to obtain six scholars in Providence."

Six wasn't enough for a school, but it was a start. By the time Prudence stepped through her own front door the following Saturday evening, it looked as if the new Crandall school for African-American girls was going to become a reality.

Of course, after the uproar over Sarah, Prudence had to be careful. She still didn't dare tell most of the people in Canterbury what she was planning. It was too soon for that. But it was hard to stay quiet. Her ideas for the new school were exciting, and on Monday she told her good friend the factory owner Daniel Packer all about it.

He wasn't enthusiastic. Opening a school for young black women was certainly a "praiseworthy" project, Mr. Packer said, but it might not work. Prudence might not be able to get enough pupils. The school might fail. He was afraid Prudence might "injure [herself] in the undertaking."

Prudence had to admit that Packer had a point. She did need more students. So she packed a bag, boarded a steamboat, and headed off to New York to recruit a few more pupils.

Thanks to letters of introduction from William Lloyd Garrison and the help of a local black minister, the trip was a success. In a few days Prudence had signed up a total of twenty students from Providence, New York, Boston, and Philadelphia.

And that wasn't all. On the boat back to Connecticut, she struck up a conversation with a middle-aged New York businessman named Arthur Tappan. Tappan was rich. He was also a passionate abolitionist. Like his famous ancestor, Benjamin Franklin, he believed African Americans should be educated. He listened to Prudence's plans and offered to help in any way he could. He even teased her a little. Maybe he'd come to school along with her other pupils, he said.

There was only one thing left to do. As soon as she got home, Prudence told her family about her plans. She knew they opposed slavery. She knew they believed in educating women. But how would they feel about the risk Prudence was taking? How would they feel about having their daughter open a school for black girls? Would they think the whole project was a crazy gamble? One brother, Reuben, had serious doubts. Prudence's father, Pardon, was afraid it might interfere with his "peace and quietness." Still, on the whole, the family approved.

Things were going even better than Prudence might have expected. The pieces were falling into place. The building was ready. The students were waiting. All Prudence had to do now was open the new school.

Chapter 4

"Moses Had a Black Wife"

ON A CHILLY DAY IN FEBRUARY, Prudence told her white students that their classes at the Crandall school were about to end. At the beginning of the spring term, she explained, her school would accept only African-American pupils.

The news swept through town.

On the night of February 24, four of the "most powerful men" in Canterbury held an emergency meeting to discuss Prudence's new school. The two lawyers in the group, Daniel Frost, Jr., and Rufus Adams, were joined by the town physician, Dr. Andrew Harris, and by Richard Fenner, one of Canterbury's most important businessmen. All four agreed that the situation was dangerous, and they rapidly formulated a plan.

In this recent photo the front door of the Crandall schoolhouse looks as it may have looked on that February day when "the most powerful men" in Canterbury came to tell Prudence they would destroy her school.

At nine A.M. the next morning, they were standing on Prudence's doorstep. She invited them in. As they sat in her parlor, stiff and formal in their starched shirts and dark coats, Prudence scanned their faces. She knew them all. Mr. Frost, Mr. Adams, and Dr. Harris were on the school's board of visitors. Dr. Harris, who lived across the street, had helped teach her brother Reuben medicine. Mr. Adams was Canterbury's justice of the peace, and Mr. Frost had founded a temperance society to prevent people from drinking alcohol. They were all prominent citizens, and Prudence must have suspected that the visit had something to do with her project.

The men didn't keep her in suspense for long. They had come to deliver a warning: If Prudence Crandall opened a school for African Americans in Canterbury, they would "do everything in their power to *destroy* [the] undertaking."

The words were brutal. The attack was alarming.

Prudence had never faced such malice before. She needed advice, and she needed it fast. When her visitors left, she seized her pen and dashed off a letter to the Reverend Simeon Jocelyn, an abolitionist minister she'd met through William Lloyd Garrison. Only a couple of years earlier, in 1831, the Reverend Jocelyn had faced a similar predicament. He'd almost been assaulted by an angry mob when he tried to open a school for African-American men in New Haven, Connecticut. Maybe he could help. Prudence's pen sped over the paper. "Mr. Jocelyn, Sir," she wrote, "your opinion and advice will be THANKFULLY received. . . . Write to me IMMEDIATELY. . . . Please write me IMMEDIATELY."

The days sped by. Then on March 1 there was another knock. Dr. Harris, Mr. Frost, Mr. Adams, and Mr. Fenner were on the doorstep again. Minutes later the men were in the school parlor. They had something to say.

Daniel Frost, a good, persuasive speaker, acted as spokesman. Now, as the other men sat silently, he tried to talk Prudence into giving up her plan to open a school for black girls. There were no threats this time. Instead, his tone was quiet and reasonable. He had no objection to educating black people, Frost explained. He just didn't want to educate them in his hometown.

It was important for Miss Crandall to understand, he

said, that opening a school for blacks was a bad idea. For one thing, it might encourage African Americans to think they were just as good as white people. That was dangerous, he said, because there was no telling what such uppity black folks might do. They might hurt whites and damage property. Worst of all, they might want to marry white Americans.

As Mr. Frost talked on, Prudence remembered a Bible story. In the book of Exodus she'd read that Moses had married a woman with a dark complexion. Apparently, the great Jewish leader had cared about skin color less than the four annoying small-town notables sitting in her parlor did.

The more Frost talked, the more absurd his ideas seemed, and Prudence had had enough. As her visitor babbled on about the dangers of letting blacks and whites marry, Prudence said sharply, "Moses had a black wife."

The words were startling. Saying them was scandalous. Nineteenth-century women were supposed to be gentle, submissive creatures who always obeyed men. But instead of meekly accepting the opinions of her male visitors, Prudence had talked back. With a single cutting remark, she'd shown that Frost's arguments about race were unfounded and ridiculous. It was a shocking, unladylike thing to do. And it wasn't something her male visitors were likely to forgive or forget.

Chapter 5

"Will Not You . . . Be My Attorney?"

On Saturday, March 2, 1833, readers of the *Liberator* noticed a small advertisement neatly tucked in the far right column of the paper. It said:

PRUDENCE CRANDALL

PRINCIPAL OF THE CANTERBURY, (CONN.) FEMALE BOARDING SCHOOL

Returns her most sincere thanks to those who have patronized her School, and would give information that on the first Monday of April next, her School will be opened for the reception of young Ladies and little Misses of color. The branches taught are as follows: Reading, Writing, Arithmetic, English Grammar, Geography, History, Natural and

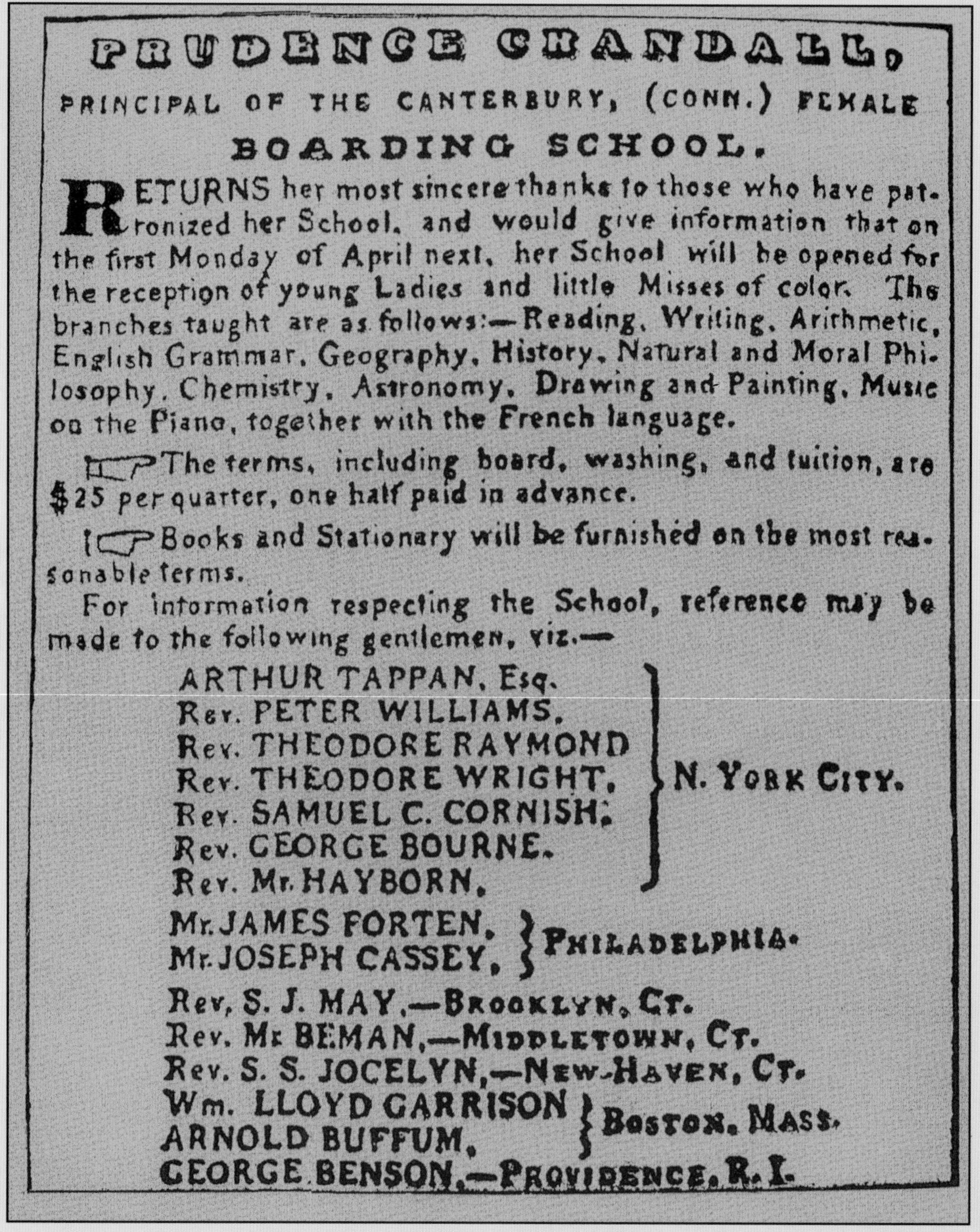

PRUDENCE CRANDALL,

PRINCIPAL OF THE CANTERBURY, (CONN.) FEMALE BOARDING SCHOOL.

RETURNS her most sincere thanks to those who have patronized her School, and would give information that on the first Monday of April next, her School will be opened for the reception of young Ladies and little Misses of color. The branches taught are as follows:—Reading, Writing, Arithmetic, English Grammar, Geography, History, Natural and Moral Philosophy, Chemistry, Astronomy, Drawing and Painting, Music on the Piano, together with the French language.

The terms, including board, washing, and tuition, are $25 per quarter, one half paid in advance.

Books and Stationary will be furnished on the most reasonable terms.

For information respecting the School, reference may be made to the following gentlemen, viz.—

ARTHUR TAPPAN, Esq.
Rev. PETER WILLIAMS,
Rev. THEODORE RAYMOND
Rev. THEODORE WRIGHT,
Rev. SAMUEL C. CORNISH,
Rev. GEORGE BOURNE,
Rev. Mr. HAYBORN,
} N. YORK CITY.

Mr. JAMES FORTEN,
Mr. JOSEPH CASSEY,
} PHILADELPHIA.

Rev. S. J. MAY,—BROOKLYN, CT.
Rev. Mr BEMAN,—MIDDLETOWN, CT.
Rev. S. S. JOCELYN,—NEW-HAVEN, CT.
Wm. LLOYD GARRISON
ARNOLD BUFFUM,
} BOSTON, MASS.
GEORGE BENSON,—PROVIDENCE, R.I.

The advertisement for Prudence's school that appeared in the *Liberator*.

Moral Philosophy, Chemistry, Astronomy, Drawing and Painting, Music on the Piano, together with the French language.

Nearby, under the headline "High School for Young Colored Ladies and Misses" was an article announcing the opening of Prudence's new school. It said she was a well qualified teacher who "richly deserved" a large number of pupils. It also said that Canterbury was a very "pleasant" place.

But "pleasant" wasn't the right word. At the moment, Canterbury was anything but pleasant because the people who lived in that small Connecticut town were furious.

By March 4, indignant citizens had already held three meetings to complain about the opening of Prudence's new school, and they were nailing up signs announcing that another big town protest meeting would be held on Saturday, March 9. The residents were so angry and prejudice against blacks in town was so violent that antislavery lecturer Arnold Buffum was told to stay away from Canterbury. It wouldn't be safe for him to show his face in town, friends said.

But not everyone in Connecticut was angry or antiblack. Six miles from Canterbury, in the town of Brooklyn, Unitarian minister Samuel May was horrified by the fury. May was a gentle man with a kindly face, an iron will, and a passionate hatred of injustice. As a little boy, he had loved the black woman who cared for him. As an adult, he had made up his mind to fight slavery and racism. But the decision hadn't been easy. Angry churchgoers almost fired May after he preached his first antislavery sermon. Even his own family thought the passionate young minister's ideas were muddled and dangerous. Steer clear of "that wrong-headed fanatical Mr. Garrison," May's father told his son. Don't try to "overthrow the system of slavery." But May didn't listen. Instead, he joined abolitionist societies. He made friends with the "fanatical" William Lloyd Garrison. He told his congregation that slavery was evil. When he heard about the new school, May sent Prudence a letter right away. "Miss Crandall," he wrote,

Although I am a stranger to you, I shall offer no apology for addressing you. . . .

Last week I heard . . . that you proposed to open a boarding school for colored girls. The intelligence rejoiced my heart, and I determined to do all in my power to assist you.

For Prudence, that letter was better than a Christmas present. In Canterbury everyone seemed to be set against her, and she needed friends badly. When May's letter arrived, Prudence sent back an answer. Would you please visit me as soon as possible? she asked.

Almost as soon as he finished reading the letter, May headed for Canterbury.

Samuel Joseph May, Prudence's good friend and advisor, as he looked in the 1850s.

He had barely entered the town when several Canterbury citizens stopped him. If May was a friend of Miss Crandall's, he'd better watch out, they said. There was no telling what might happen to someone who wanted to help the schoolteacher.

Samuel May ignored the threat and rode straight to Prudence's house.

To his surprise, Prudence was calm. Her thoughts were logical and her voice was steady. But she had a serious problem. It was Monday. The big Saturday town meeting was only five days away, and Prudence did not have a spokesman who could present her views at the gathering.

She couldn't go to the meeting herself. That was clear. It was 1833. Women did not have the right to vote. They could not hold public office, and they were not allowed to participate in public meetings. Most men—and some women—thought it was rude or indecent for a female to speak up, even in private. At the Canterbury Temperance Society, women members were not allowed to address the meeting directly. They had to whisper ideas to the chairman, who then presented their thoughts to the rest of the group. Even the famed nineteenth-century teacher and author Catherine Beecher, who fought long and hard for women's education, believed that women should never get involved in conflicts or disputes. A woman who becomes a "combatant" (a fighter), she wrote, gives up the right to be protected by men.

If Prudence went to that meeting, it would be a scandal. If she stood up to debate the issues and defend her school, people would be shocked. Even the few Canterbury citizens who weren't angry about the plan to open an African-American school might be furious if Prudence dared to act in such an unladylike fashion. She couldn't risk making more enemies. But she needed someone to protect her interests at the meeting. Turning to the minister, Prudence asked, "Will not you, Friend May, . . . be my attorney?" "Certainly," May replied, "come what will."

That settled, Prudence and May began to work out their strategy. What solutions could they support at the meeting?

What could they discuss? What might be accepted? Prudence was reasonable. She was determined to open a school for black girls. That wasn't negotiable. But she was willing to move the school. If someone bought her present house in the center of town, Prudence was willing to buy another in an out-of-the-way place. That way her current neighbors—like Dr. Harris and Andrew Judson—wouldn't have to worry about having black student boarders living right next door. It seemed like a sensible plan, and May agreed to present it at the Saturday meeting.

For the next few days, Prudence considered her situation. May was on her side, but more help wouldn't hurt. The question was, where to find it? Most of the people in Canterbury wouldn't lift a finger to help. Garrison was busy putting out the *Liberator* in Boston. Her father, Pardon Crandall, would support her, but he was a farmer, not an experienced public speaker. Still, there was one other possibility. Arnold Buffum, a friend of Garrison's who worked as a lecturer for the New-England Anti-Slavery Society, was speaking in a nearby town that week. He seemed like a good prospect. Of course, time was short, but Prudence knew how to get things done. On Friday, March 8, she tied on her bonnet and traveled out to talk to Buffum. Although friends had told him it was unsafe for an abolitionist to visit

Canterbury, Buffum ignored the warning. He promised Prudence that he would be at the big town meeting.

By the time she went to bed on Friday night, Prudence could be proud of the way she'd handled her problem. She hadn't backed down. She hadn't panicked. She had rounded up two respected, intelligent, practiced public speakers to present her point of view. She'd planned a strategy. She had done everything she could reasonably do to get ready for the town meeting.

But was it enough?

The Canterbury Congregational church where the town meeting was held. Detail from a print showing Canterbury in the nineteenth century.

Chapter 6

"Men of Canterbury. . . . Hear Me!"

THE HOURS TICKED by on Saturday afternoon. The sun went down. The night was cool. As he made his way through the darkened Canterbury streets, Reverend Samuel May must have been an anxious man. In a little while he had to speak at the town meeting. Somehow he had to talk a roomful of angry, prejudiced citizens into letting Prudence open her school. He was willing to do the job. There was no question about that. But persuading that hostile Canterbury crowd to change its mind was going to be a little like trying to stop a cattle stampede single-handedly.

It wasn't quite time for the meeting, and May stopped at the Crandall house to make a few last-minute arrangements. When Prudence ushered him into the parlor, the clergyman was surprised to find Arnold Buffum there. Buffum, an experienced speaker, was a valuable ally, and May was delighted to hear that he would also be representing Prudence at the meeting. The two men waited while Prudence handed each of them a letter addressed to the meeting chairman. The letters said that May and Buffum were acting as her spokesmen, and that she would abide by any decision they made.

It was getting late. The men had to leave. Prudence escorted her visitors into the front hall, showed them out, and closed the door. There was nothing she could do now but trust her friends and wait.

Together, May and Buffum crossed the road and joined the crowd of men streaming toward the brightly lit Congregational church where the meeting was to be held.

Inside, the church was jammed. Almost a thousand people were packed into the downstairs pews and upstairs balconies. May and Buffum slipped into seats on the ground floor, close to the front, and waited. The moderator called the meeting to order. The rustling and talk subsided, and Rufus Adams rose to speak. His message was simple. Opening a school for black girls in Canterbury, he said, would damage the "persons, property and reputations of [its] citizens." The townsfolk had to protest, he said. They had to tell the Crandall woman to stop.

As the crowd digested this, Andrew T. Judson took the floor. Everybody in Canterbury knew Judson. The thin-lipped lawyer with the bushy, dark side-whiskers was one of the richest, most important men in town. He was a member of the Connecticut state legislature, a bank director, a possible candidate for governor, and a former member of the Crandall school's board of visitors. He also lived right across the street from Prudence's house. Mr. Judson was used to speaking to big groups, and he began to stir up the crowd.

Andrew Judson, Prudence's foe, was a man generally known for his "tact and courtesy."

The school was a "calamity," Judson said. In fact, the very idea of having "a school of nigger girls so near him was insupportable." If that school opened, Judson thundered, Canterbury's "sons and daughters would be forever ruined" and "property [would] be no longer safe." For the sake of the "honor" of the town, he did not want one single, precious corner of Canterbury "appropriated to such a purpose."

The crowd roared with approval. Judson bowed, and May and Buffum knew they had to reply. They handed Prudence's letters to Rufus Adams and asked permission to speak. Adams passed the letters on to Judson, who glanced at the papers and leaped to his feet. Turning to May and Buffum, he blasted the two men for daring to interfere. Since they didn't live in Canterbury, it was against the law for the two abolitionists to speak at a town meeting, Judson said. How dare they talk about Miss Crandall and her school? It was none of their confounded business.

That did it. The crowd exploded. People screamed. Men shook their fists at May and Buffum and yelled that the two outsiders were breaking the law.

Trapped, Prudence's two spokesmen sat still, probably wondering if they were going to be beat up or thrown in jail.

One man, raising his voice above the roar, suggested that Canterbury solve the problem by buying Prudence's house and letting her move the school to some other place. He was promptly shouted down.

A vote was taken. The crowd resolved to protest the school, and, at last, the chairman adjourned the meeting.

That was May's chance. If the meeting was over, he couldn't be accused of breaking the law by speaking.

Jumping up onto a chair, he bellowed, "Men of Canterbury! I have a word for you! Hear me!"

Half the crowd turned to listen. Pitching his voice so he could be heard in the big hall, May tried to tell the men that Prudence's African-American students were good, responsible girls. The school was not going to ruin the town, he said; it was only going to educate children. Buffum tried to add a few words, but he'd barely opened his mouth when Judson loudly ordered everyone out of the building. "Out! Out!" screamed a group of men, as they drove people out of the church and slammed the doors behind them.

May and Buffum stayed outside, talking to anybody who would listen. The crowd gradually drifted away, and finally even Prudence's friends headed home to their beds.

But the fireworks weren't over.

A week after the meeting, *Liberator* readers found an account of the events at the Canterbury town meeting in the paper under the furious headline "Heathenism Outdone!"

In Canterbury, four men visited the Crandall house to tell Prudence that the people at the meeting wanted her to abolish the school. Instead of answering her visitors directly, Prudence responded by letter. In quiet, dignified words she said that before making a decision she would have to consult her friends.

But the most surprising event occurred two days after the uproar in the church, when Andrew Judson paid a call on Samuel May. The lawyer said he had come to apologize. He hoped there were no hard feelings. Still, he wanted May to know that a "nigger school [would] never be allowed in Canterbury, nor in any town [in Connecticut]."

"How can you prevent it . . .?" May retorted.

"We can expel her pupils under the . . . [current] laws." Or, said Judson, "we will get a [new] law passed by our Leglislature"—a law that would prevent black children from other states from attending school in Connecticut.

May threatened to fight.

"You talk big," Judson snapped, but fighting those laws in court "will cost more than you are aware."

Yes, May responded, that was true. He didn't personally have the money to fight unjust laws in the courts, but other people did. In fact, May added, he was sure that "lovers of impartial liberty" would donate money to stop Judson's "attempt to crush by legal means, the Canterbury school."

Unable to reply, Judson turned on his heel and stormed out of the house.

When May saw Prudence several days later, he told her that the situation was dangerous and the choices were plain. If she was scared of men like Judson, she had to quit. If she still wanted to open the school, May would stand by her.

Prudence, however, seemed to be thriving on the conflict. "In the midst of this affliction I am as happy as at any moment in my life," she wrote to her abolitionist friend the Reverend Simeon Jocelyn several weeks after the meeting.

Prudence had made up her mind. She was going to open the new school, and she had to get ready for her pupils.

Chapter 7

"Miss Crandall Has Commenced Her School"

It was the first Monday in April. Opening day. The books were on the shelves. The schoolroom was ready. Prudence and her younger sister and assistant, Almira, were waiting to welcome twenty new students.

But by five o'clock that afternoon Prudence had only two pupils: Sarah Harris, her original black student, and Eliza Glasko, the daughter of a prosperous blacksmith from Griswold, Connecticut.

Still, the arrival of those two teenage black girls upset the neighbors. Andrew Judson and his friends called another town meeting to deal with this problem, and the men at this meeting decided to send a petition to the Connecticut legislature, asking lawmakers to make it illegal for blacks from other states to come to Connecticut. That, the townsfolk felt, would keep other African-American students from coming to Canterbury in the future.

But what about the two black students who were already at the Crandall school? Something had to be done about them, and the men at the meeting wanted action. To punish Prudence, to show her how they felt, and, above all, to stop her from enrolling more students, they decided to start a type of strike called a boycott. Most of the shopkeepers in Canterbury agreed not to sell groceries or supplies to Prudence. It would be pretty hard, they figured, for her to live—or run a boarding school—without being able to buy basic provisions like sugar, flour, paper, medicine, or meat in town.

And that was only the beginning.

In the days that followed the meeting, a neighbor told Prudence's father that a mob might tear down his house. When Prudence and her students stepped out onto the street, Canterbury hooligans shouted rude remarks and threw stones, eggs, chicken heads, and bits of manure at the girls.

The only bright note came from the *Liberator*. "We have received," Garrison wrote, "the heart-cheering information that Miss Crandall has commenced her school, and is resolved to persevere against all opposition."

1839] *Anti-Slavery Almanac.* 15

COLORED SCHOOLS BROKEN UP, IN THE FREE STATES.

When schools have been established for colored scholars, the law-makers and the mob have combined to destroy them;—as at Canterbury, Ct., at Canaan, N. H., Aug. 10, 1835, at Zanesville and Brown Co., Ohio, in 1836.

IMMEDIATE EMANCIPATION.

Aug. 1, 1834, 30,000 slaves were emancipated in Antigua. Without any apprenticeship, or system of preparation, preceding the act, the chains were broken at a stroke, and they all went out FREE! It is now four years since these 30,000 slaves were "turned loose" among 2,000 whites, their former masters. These masters fought against the emancipation bill with all their force and fury. They remonstrated with the British Government—conjured and threatened,—protested that emancipation would ruin the island, that the emancipated slaves would never work—would turn vagabonds, butcher the whites and flood the island with beggary and crime. Their strong beseechings availed as little as their threats, and croakings about ruin. The Emancipation Act, unintimidated by the bluster, traversed quietly through its successive stages up to the royal sanction, and became the law of the land. When the slaveholders of Antigua saw that abolition was *inevitable*, they at once resolved to substitute immediate, unconditional, and entire emancipation for the gradual process contemplated by the Act. Well, what has been the result? Read the following testimony of the very men who, but little more than four years ago, denounced and laughed to scorn the idea of abolishing

Print from an 1839 antislavery publication showing a white mob attacking a school like Prudence's. In addition to the assault on the Crandall school, such mobs attacked at least two other schools for African Americans in northern states during the 1830s. (In one case, three hundred armed men used oxen to drag a building that had been used as a black school into a nearby swamp.)

In a classroom in the elegant white schoolhouse at the center of town, lessons began. Sarah and Eliza tried to work at their books. Prudence tried to concentrate on teaching, but there were so many distractions. She had to worry about the insults, the petition, the boycott, whether her father and brother could haul enough supplies to the school from out of town to keep it going, and—on top of all that—there was the problem of pupils. She couldn't keep the school open long with only two students. If the other girls she'd recruited didn't turn up soon, her school would be bankrupt.

Still, April 12 was a good day. A new pupil, seventeen-year-old Ann Eliza Hammond, arrived from Providence. She was the first student from outside Connecticut, and the town knew it.

The next evening, at about seven P.M. the Canterbury sheriff pounded on the Crandall door. He'd come to deliver a written warning from the town authorities. It said that Prudence and Ann Eliza were breaking the law.

It was an old law, one that most people in Canterbury probably didn't know existed. Originally written in 1650 to keep homeless beggars out of town, the ordinance had been dredged up by Andrew Judson and his friends. In simple terms, it said that all visitors from other states had to get permission from the town authorities to stay in Canterbury.

Ann Eliza was from Rhode Island. The Canterbury authorities had not given her permission to stay in town. If she did not leave immediately, the warning said, Prudence would be fined $1.68 for every week her student stayed in school. If Prudence did not pay the fine, Ann Eliza would be arrested, sent to the town whipping post, and "whipped on the naked body not exceeding ten stripes."

That was serious and frightening. There was no way Prudence would ever allow Ann Eliza to be whipped, but what could she do? A fine of $1.68 didn't sound like a lot of money, but it would mount up. In four weeks it would be enough to pay a female schoolteacher's monthly salary. In thirteen weeks it would add up to almost as much as Prudence was charging Ann Eliza for a quarter's tuition. Worse still, if Prudence paid Ann Eliza's fines and the fines for every other out-of-state pupil who came to the school, she'd soon be penniless.

Prudence needed help, and once again her friends provided it. Several wealthy abolitionists promised to pay the town up to ten thousand dollars in possible student fines, and May himself made a special trip to Canterbury to tell the girls not to be frightened. The whipping was only a threat, he explained. He was sure the town authorities would never dare carry it out. After all, May said, beating

Two antislavery tokens from the 1830s showing bound slaves and bearing the legends "Am I not a man and a brother?" and "Am I not a woman and a sister?" Contributions from wealthy supporters (like Arthur Tappan) allowed abolitionists to advertise their beliefs with songs, pamphlets, and even tokens like these. Although tokens were made privately, they were sometimes used as money. These would have been worth about one cent.

children who had committed no real crime was an act that would horrify the entire "land, if not . . . the whole civilized world."

To his surprise, however, Ann Eliza didn't seem to need reassurance. She was calm and determined. The only thing that mattered to her was getting an education. To help the school, she was ready to put up with injuries, insults, and even a public whipping.

Despite the difficulties, new students kept arriving. One girl, from Hartford, Connecticut, was treated so badly by the other passengers on the stagecoach that she got off in Brooklyn, picked up her baggage, and hiked the remaining six miles to Canterbury.

Six pupils arrived from New York, and more came from Pennsylvania, Rhode Island, and Massachusetts. One girl was the daughter of a freed slave. Another, who offered to do housework to pay for her education, had her fees partially paid by a hard-up white abolitionist clergyman. A third was sent to school by a friendly former slave who had purchased her own freedom.

There were now enough students to make a real class. Prudence lectured. The girls concentrated on their reading and arithmetic. In the classroom it was calm and quiet. But if the girls stepped outside the front gate, boys tailed after them blowing horns, beating drums, and shouting insults. Someone smeared dung on the school steps and door handles, and the doors and windows were pelted by volleys of rotten eggs. Most of the shopkeepers stuck by their agreement and would not sell Prudence supplies. The milk peddler refused to deliver fresh milk, and a local newspaper accused Prudence of trying to "break down the barriers which God has placed between blacks and whites."

The troubles came so thick and fast, it was hard to count them all. Opening the school had been a hundred times harder than Prudence had imagined. Of course, she'd known that some people would object to black students. She'd expected some protests, but as she explained to the Reverend Jocelyn shortly after the school opened, "The thought of such opposition as has been raised in the minds of the people of Canterbury . . . *never once entered* into my mind." She had never imagined "that Christians would act so unwisely and conduct [themselves] . . . so outrageously." Nothing had prepared her for this "present scene of adversity." But she'd made up her mind. She wasn't going to give up. "I trust God will help me keep this resolution," she wrote.

Chapter 8

"Unjust . . . and Disgraceful"

There was no question about it. Mr. Judson was a busy man. Threatening Prudence and her students with fines and a whipping hadn't forced the schoolteacher and her pupils out of Canterbury. But that didn't matter. There were other ways to destroy the school, and Andrew T. Judson had a plan.

He knew the school couldn't stay open without students, and he knew that most of Prudence's pupils came from outside Connecticut. If he could stop the out-of-state students from coming, the school would have to close. And that was just what Mr. Judson wanted.

At the last Canterbury town meeting, participants had decided to send a petition to the Connecticut legislature, asking it to pass a law that would specifically prevent African Americans who lived in other states from visiting Connecticut. Now, Mr. Judson was hard at work collecting signatures for that petition. In Brooklyn (where the Reverend May lived), 118 people signed. In nearby Plainfield, 81 more added their names. One hundred and thirty-one Canterbury residents signed on, and people in thirteen other towns put down their signatures. Day by day the numbers grew. In a few weeks, Andrew Judson had a petition with 903 signatures to take to the Connecticut legislature in Hartford.

Nine hundred and three wasn't a huge number. It certainly wasn't a majority of the people living in Connecticut, but the state legislators took the petition seriously. Fearing that the existence of a school for African Americans would encourage blacks from other parts of the United States to move into Connecticut, they began to draw up a law that would stop African-American students who lived in other states from going to school in Connecticut.

At home in Canterbury, Prudence, her pupils, and her assistant teacher, William Burleigh, tried to carry on. They had lessons. They worked. When the spring breeze blew through the windows, they must have tried not to notice that the curtains had been stained by barrages of rotten eggs.

Since Prudence refused to cower in her house, she took the girls on an outing to the nearby town of Norwich. Despite the gangs of boys who sometimes threw sticks and stones at the students, Prudence and her charges made the trip safely. But life was hard. Although a few Canterbury shopkeepers continued to sell the school groceries, Prudence's father and her oldest brother, Hezekiah, often had to buy supplies in other towns and cart them to the school by wagon. In Hartford the legislature continued to work on the new law that Prudence knew was aimed at keeping students out of her school. A whole army seemed to be lined up against her, and it was time to fight back.

Prudence knew, of course, that proper, well-brought-up nineteenth-century ladies were supposed to bear their troubles silently, but she couldn't afford to worry about such convention. For weeks her enemies had been stirring up anger and spreading lies about her school, and Prudence had to tell her side of the story.

She did it as politely as she could. In a calm, well-written letter to a local newspaper, Prudence laid out the facts. She told readers how she'd originally met Sarah Harris, why she'd decided to start the school, and why she felt it was important to fight against prejudice, "the mother of all abominations." She also told readers that the school had only one purpose: to "instruct the ignorant and . . . prepare teachers for the people of color."

It was a good, clear, sensible letter, but it didn't change a lot of minds in Canterbury. It didn't stop Andrew Judson, and it didn't stop the Connecticut state legislature from planning the new law against African Americans.

Hezekiah Crandall, Prudence's older brother, who hauled supplies to the school even though he knew that helping his sister might hurt his business.

Still, Prudence did have friends. The Reverend May supplied advice. Simeon Jocelyn encouraged her, and Prudence soon came to depend on Samuel May's Brooklyn neighbors, the Benson family. George Benson, a rich, retired abolitionist merchant, was a good friend of William Lloyd Garrison's, and his children, particularly his daughters, Anna, Helen, and Mary, became some of Prudence's dearest friends.

Luckily, Prudence could also count on her own family. One brother, Reuben, wanted his sister to close the school, but the other Crandalls stood staunchly by her side.

Esther Crandall, Prudence's mother. Despite threats, Prudence's parents supported their daughter's school.

Prudence's sister, Almira, continued to help with the teaching chores. Hezekiah took time off from running his cotton mill to bring her supplies, and her father, Pardon, stuck by his stubborn daughter. "My family was the setters up of that school and myself a supporter of that family," he said when people asked about the situation. A farmer and part-time village schoolmaster, Pardon believed in fairness and freedom. When he heard that the legislature was trying to keep black students out of Connecticut, he instantly wrote to the lawmakers, urging them not to "destroy any of the rights of free people . . . whether they are black or white."

It was a waste of ink.

On May 24, 1833, the legislature passed a statute that became known as the Connecticut Black Law. It said, "No person [in Connecticut] shall set up . . . [a] school . . . for the . . . education of colored persons who are not inhabitants of this State." That meant it was illegal for African-American students from other states to go to Connecticut schools. A Connecticut citizen—like Prudence—could be jailed or fined for running or supporting a school that admitted out-of-state black students. And the fines were huge: $100 for the first offense, $200 for the second, $400 for the third, and so on. If Prudence had seven students from outside Connecticut, her fines would amount to $6,400. She could never pay a sum like that. If the Canterbury authorities enforced the law, Prudence and the school would be ruined.

It was just what Andrew Judson and his friends wanted. To celebrate the new law, the Canterbury townsfolk fired off a cannon thirteen times. Then they shot rifles into the air, danced around bonfires, and kept the church bells clanging for hours.

Other U.S. citizens reacted differently. Unprejudiced people were appalled by the new Black Law—and said so. In Hartford a local newspaper condemned the statute. In New York an abolitionist newspaper called the *Emancipator* printed a stinging letter that called the law "unjust . . . and disgraceful." A group of Connecticut citizens even sent a petition to their legislature, asking that the lawmakers repeal the statute immediately.

But criticism didn't bother Andrew Judson. As soon as the new statute was on the books, Mr. Judson and the Canterbury justice of the peace drove out to the Crandall farm. From now on, they told Pardon, carrying groceries and supplies to his daughter's school was strictly against the law. Make no mistake about it, they told the old man: "If you go to your daughter's you are to be fined $100 for the first offense, $200 for the second, and double it every time." Then they turned to Prudence's mother. "Mrs. Crandall," they said, "if you go there, you will be fined. . . . And your daughter (the one who established the school for colored females) . . . will be . . . put in jail, in close confinement. . . . There is no mercy to be shown about it."

Pardon Crandall listened to the two men, but he had no intention of letting them tell him what to do. He didn't like being bullied. He believed Prudence had a right to run her school. Besides, no one was going to stop him from visiting or helping his daughter. Still, even Pardon had to admit that the situation was dangerous. The new law had been passed. The penalties were severe, and sooner or later Judson and the Canterbury authorities were going to carry out their threats.

In the schoolhouse, Prudence gathered her pupils around her. She had thirteen students now. They were happy and

Room in the Crandall house today showing the kind of globe that Prudence and her students might have used for geography lessons. Prudence hoped that such lessons would prepare her girls to teach other African-American children.

doing well in their studies, and she still had ads in the *Liberator* asking for more pupils. When he visited, the Reverend May found that Prudence and the girls looked "calm and resolute." Years later, however, Prudence would confess that these were "weary, weary" days. She had no intention of closing the school, but she knew it would be hard to fight the new law, and it wasn't easy to figure out exactly what would happen next.

Chapter 9

"SAVAGE BARBARITY!"

JUNE CAME. Children ran barefoot in the grass. Wildflowers sprouted in the meadows, and two representatives of the Canterbury town authorities rapped sharply on the Crandall school door. Prudence asked what they wanted. Just the answer to a simple question, the men said: Did Miss Crandall have black students from outside Connecticut in her classroom?

Prudence answered honestly. Yes, she told the visitors, she had a number of students from other states. Then she introduced the men to several girls who had come from outside Connecticut.

The men listened quietly and left. Still, Prudence must have guessed that the next time the town authorities came,

A recent photo of the front door of the Crandall schoolhouse. Prudence once opened this door to a steady stream of students, friends, officials, and enemies.

the encounter might not be as pleasant.

As always, Prudence discussed the situation with her good friend the Reverend May. Together they agreed that sometime soon the Canterbury authorities were likely to arrest Prudence for breaking the new Black Law. The question was, what to do when it happened? Should May and Prudence's other abolitionist friends prevent her from going to prison by promptly paying bail? Or, should she go to jail—at least briefly—to attract public attention and show, as the Reverend May explained, "how bad, how wicked, how cruel" the new law really was? After reviewing the options carefully, Prudence and Samuel May made their plans.

It was lucky they did.

A few days later, on June 27, there was another visitor at the Crandall door. This time it was the Canterbury deputy sheriff. He had a warrant to arrest Prudence Crandall for the crime of teaching "colored persons, who . . . were not inhabitants of any town in this state."

It was exactly what Prudence and May had expected. When she saw the officer, Prudence stayed calm. She didn't protest. Instead, she quietly accompanied the deputy to the house of the local magistrate. There, while Andrew Judson and several other men looked on, justice of the peace Rufus Adams read out the charges. Are you guilty or not guilty? he asked Prudence.

"Not guilty," she replied.

Her trial would be held in August. Until then, Adams said, Prudence had a choice: she could stay in prison awaiting the trial date, or she could live at home after paying $150 in bail. Prudence didn't hesitate. She had discussed this situation with May, and she knew exactly what her answer would be. In a cool, dignified manner she told the men that she didn't have enough money to pay the bail. She would have to go to prison.

Go to prison?

Judson and Adams could hardly believe their ears. Of

course, they had issued the arrest warrant. They had hoped to frighten the pesky teacher into closing her school. But they'd never actually intended to send Prudence to jail. Now they were trapped. Since Prudence wouldn't pay the bail, they had to put a nice, respectable young woman in prison for teaching children. That was embarrassing. It made them look cruel, and it might even make people feel sorry for Miss Crandall.

Somehow Judson and his friends had to find a way to keep Prudence out of prison.

Before noon, a messenger from the Canterbury town authorities was banging on Samuel May's door. Inside, the courier gasped out that Prudence "was in the hands of the sheriff and would be put into jail" unless May and her other friends immediately paid $150 in bail.

Reverend May listened. He remembered the plans he'd made with Prudence. Then he shook his head. No, he told the messenger. He wouldn't pay the bail.

"But sir," babbled the messenger, "do you mean her to be put in jail?"

"Most certainly," May replied, "if her persecutors [enemies] . . . let such an outrage be committed."

There was nothing Judson and the Canterbury authorities

could do. They had arrested Prudence. No one was willing to pay her bail. Now, like it or not, they had to put the schoolteacher in prison.

Reluctantly, Sheriff Roger Coit escorted Prudence to a carriage and started to drive her to the Brooklyn jail. By then, news of the arrest had spread through town, and curious people had gathered by the roadside to watch the famous Miss Crandall ride off to prison.

When the carriage drew up at the two-story gray stone jail, May was waiting. He had spent the afternoon making sure that Prudence's cell was clean and equipped with good bedding. Still, despite his work, the prison was a dismal place, and May was afraid Prudence might lose her nerve when she saw it. As she dismounted from the carriage, he leaned forward and whispered, "If . . . you hesitate, if you dread the gloomy place so much as to wish to be saved from it, I will give [bail] for you . . . now."

"Oh no," Prudence replied. "I am only afraid they will *not* put me into jail."

Still, the sheriff delayed. He chatted with the bystanders. He seemed to be hoping that someone would turn up with the bail money, but no one offered to pay.

Soon it was sunset. The sheriff couldn't stall any longer. He handed Prudence over to the jailer, who politely escorted her to a cell. But she didn't have to stay there alone. Anna Benson, one of Prudence's closest abolitionist friends, had volunteered to stay in prison with her.

May waited until he heard the cell door lock, then headed home, leaving the two women alone in the barred room.

Luckily, they didn't have to stay there long. May and Prudence had agreed that she would stay in jail just long enough to create a sensation. By four o'clock the following afternoon, Anna's abolitionist father, George Benson, had paid the bail as planned. By evening, both women were safely home, and newspapers were starting to spread the story of Prudence's ordeal.

"SAVAGE BARBARITY! Miss Crandall Imprisoned!!!" thundered the *Liberator*. The *Female Advocate* angrily condemned Andrew Judson for throwing "FEMALES INTO PRISON FOR SEEKING FEMALE IMPROVEMENT AND ELEVATION." When he heard the news, the famous American poet John Greenleaf Whittier was appalled. Writing in the *Essex Gazette,* he exclaimed: "In prison for teaching their colored sisters to read the Bible . . . Just God! Can this be possible?"

But not everyone was sympathetic. Some criticized Prudence for spending a night in jail because it was unladylike. "[Miss Crandall] has stepped out of the hallowed precincts of female propriety . . . and must expect common treatment," scolded a local newspaper. The editor of the *New York Commercial Advertiser* said that Prudence was an ignorant, easily led woman who simply obeyed strong-minded male abolitionists like William Lloyd Garrison.

Certainly, the story was a sensation. In towns and cities all over the East Coast people were talking about Prudence Crandall. Students at the Brown Seminary in Providence, Rhode Island, were even told to write compositions about her. Some pupils, however, didn't pay much attention to the assignment. One young man was so mixed up that he turned in an essay dealing with a mysterious lady named "Priscilla" Crandall.

The attention and the sympathy were welcome, but they didn't solve Prudence's basic problem. In two months, on August 22, she was going to be tried for breaking the Connecticut Black Law. Arthur Tappan, the wealthy abolitionist that Prudence had met on the way back from her student-recruiting trip to New York, had offered to pay the very best lawyers in the state to defend her. That was good news, but it was no guarantee. Even good lawyers sometimes lost in court. At the moment, only one thing was certain: if the jury found her guilty, Prudence might have to spend far more than one night in jail.

Chapter 10

Under Attack

As the summer days flew by, classes at the Crandall school continued and more pupils enrolled. By July, Prudence had about seventeen students, and the big house was crowded with boarders. People who met the girls said they were well mannered and doing well in their studies, but most of the townsfolk cared only about finding new ways to drive the Crandall students out of Canterbury.

During July, members of the Canterbury Congregational Church ordered Prudence not to send her pupils there for Sunday services. It wasn't proper to have black girls sitting in pews that should be "occupied by the white females of the parish," the church authorities told Miss Crandall in a letter.

Luckily, the Reverend Levi Kneeland, pastor of the nearby Packerville Baptist Church, was an open-minded man who gladly welcomed Prudence's pupils. Each Sunday, Pardon Crandall took some of the students down the road to the Reverend Kneeland's church, and a friend of Prudence's sent a coach and driver to transport the girls who couldn't fit in Pardon's wagon. The system worked well until one Sunday when the coachman drove the girls home. As he headed toward the river, the driver spied a gang of teenage boys waiting at the spot where he had to ford the stream. The kids looked big and rowdy. The driver smelled trouble. He ordered the girls to get out of the carriage. Then, helpless and terrified, the students stood on the bank as the gang grabbed the coach, dragged it down to the river, and dumped it—upside down—into the water.

Pardon, who was driving along the road with a wagonload of pupils, saw it happen. With a quick flick of the reins, he urged his horse past the boys, across the stream, and half a mile down the road to the schoolhouse. Once his passengers were safely inside, the old man drove back to the river, picked up the other girls, and helped drag the carriage out of the water. No one was hurt, but it was the last time Prudence's students visited the Packerville church.

Going out was dangerous, but it wasn't entirely safe to stay in. At nine o'clock one night, Prudence and her girls heard a crash and the clink of broken glass. A rock the size of a man's fist had been hurled through a windowpane in the school parlor. Another night, some Canterbury vandals pitched eggs through an open school window.

A recent photo of the view from one of the windows in the Crandall schoolhouse. Fragile panes of glass were often all that protected Prudence and her girls from the stones, eggs, and chicken heads hurled at them by neighborhood rowdies.

Prudence kept up a brave front, but the stress seemed to be taking a toll. In the middle of July she came down with a fever that left her feeling low for almost a month.

Still, the work went on. Prudence's sister, Almira, helped teach the pupils. Her father and her brother Hezekiah kept on bringing supplies. Samuel May and the Reverend

Kneeland stopped by. Even Arthur Tappan paid a surprise visit to Canterbury.

From the Reverend May, the wealthy Tappan got a complete rundown on the situation. One of the problems, the minister explained, was publicity. Local newspapers were afraid to print articles that supported Prudence or the school for fear of being attacked by the Canterbury townsfolk. The solution to that, said Tappan, was to start a brand-new paper—one that would print *all* articles about the school—both pro and con. And there was no time to waste.

In a single day, Tappan rented a printing office. May found an editor. Two weeks later a new, unbiased paper called the *Unionist* was rolling off the presses.

Before he headed back to his business in New York, Tappan had one last important errand. He stopped to visit Prudence's school.

Prudence was grateful for Tappan's friendship. There were so many times when she seemed to be stranded in a sea of enemies. The truth was, however, that Prudence may have had more supporters than she knew.

While traveling through Connecticut, a British college professor asked his stagecoach driver about the Crandall school. "For my part," said the white coachman, "I cannot see why a black skin should . . . bar any one's rising in the world; or what crime there can be" in trying to help people improve themselves through education.

Those were encouraging words, but they couldn't do much to help Prudence. Only a good attorney and a friendly jury could do that, because her trial was about to start.

Arthur Tappan, the wealthy New York abolitionist who paid Prudence's legal bills and started a newspaper to help support her cause.

Chapter 11

Miss Crandall on Trial

Early in the morning of August 22, Pardon Crandall drove his daughter and eight of her students to the Brooklyn courthouse. After weeks of waiting, Prudence was going to be tried for operating a school for African Americans who came from outside Connecticut. The eight girls had been called as witnesses.

None of the women ever described how they had felt as Pardon's wagon jounced along the road that day, but all nine must have been nervous. The girls were going to take the witness stand in a courtroom crowded with white strangers. They were going to face a battery of hostile lawyers who might trick them into saying things that could hurt their teacher, damage the school, and end their chances of getting an education. For Prudence, the entire future was on the line. If the court found her guilty, she could face jail, fines, and the loss of her school. Prudence wasn't the sort of woman who showed her fears, but it must have been hard to look calm as she made her way into the crowded courtroom.

The session was scheduled to start at nine, and the lawyers were waiting. On one side of the room the tall, dignified William Ellsworth conferred with his two assistants. Ellsworth, a U.S. congressman and one of Connecticut's finest attorneys, was there to defend Prudence. On the other side of the courtroom, in their formal frock coats, were the two prosecuting attorneys: Prudence's old enemy, Andrew Judson, and his colleague Jonathon Welch.

The presiding judge entered and took his seat. The jury was chosen. To Ellsworth, it was clear from the start that the opposition had an unfair advantage. The judge was an old business associate of Andrew Judson's who had helped the legislature write the law Prudence was accused of breaking. Prosecution lawyers were allowed to rudely refer to Prudence as "Prudy," and one juror had actually helped pass the Black Law. Getting a fair verdict from a court like that might be hard, but Ellsworth and his associates had tackled tough cases before. Patiently, they waited as the prosecution called Ann Peterson, a pupil from New York, to the stand. Ann was an out-of-state student. If she answered questions truthfully about attending the Crandall school, she might also be accused of breaking the Black Law, and Ellsworth didn't want that to happen. Before prosecutor Welch could begin his examination, Mr. Ellsworth advised the witness not to answer any questions.

That was a blow, but Welch tried anyway. Has Miss Crandall "kept a school for Colored Misses [who are] not inhabitants of the State?" he asked the girl on the stand.

Miss Peterson refused to reply.

Again the attorney tried. Has Miss Crandall "instructed any person of color other than yourself?"

Again Ann was silent.

Frustrated, Welch excused Ann and called two other out-of-state students. On Ellsworth's advice, both refused to answer.

The day was warm. The room grew hot. One after another, the witnesses took the stand. Again and again Mr. Welch asked the same questions. But no one admitted that Prudence had actually taught black girls from outside Connecticut. By the end of the first day, the prosecution hadn't made much progress.

On the second morning Mr. Welch called a new witness, student Eliza Glasko.

Like the others, Eliza refused to answer. But this time the prosecution had had enough. Mr. Welch turned to the judge. If the witness won't answer questions, she should be jailed for contempt of court, he said. The judge agreed and gave an order. The bailiff started to march Eliza off to prison, but, suddenly, William Ellsworth spoke up. He didn't want a young girl to go to jail. Besides, Eliza came from Connecticut. Even if she admitted attending the Crandall school, she couldn't be charged with breaking the Black Law. She could answer the prosecution lawyer, Ellsworth said.

Now that he had a cooperative witness, Welch hurled questions. Could Eliza show the court any students who came from outside Connecticut? She pointed to a girl from Rhode Island and to two pupils from New York.

And what were those girls taught? Mr. Welch wanted to know.

"Reading, writing, grammar; geography," Eliza answered.

That was enough. Mr. Welch called his next witness: Mary Benson, one of Prudence's friends and the sister of Anna Benson, who had shared Prudence's prison cell. Miss Benson took the oath. The spectators listened, and the attorney asked his most important question: Who taught the girls in Miss Crandall's school? Miss Benson had no choice. She had sworn to tell the truth. Reluctantly, she admitted that she had seen Prudence teaching the classes.

It was all the prosecution needed. Mr. Welch had proved that Prudence had taught black girls from out of state in her school. He had proved that she had broken the law.

Mr. Welch sat down, and Andrew Judson rose to sum up the case for the prosecution.

It was clear, he told the jury, that Miss Crandall had broken the Connecticut Black Law. Now, some people might say that that law was unfair, Judson pointed out. They might say that it took away rights from black people. But, said Judson, the law couldn't take away black rights because blacks *had no rights*. They didn't have the right to go to school, and they certainly didn't have the right to travel freely from one state to another. Why? Because, said Mr. Judson, blacks—even free blacks—were *not American citizens*.

Not American citizens?

To the jury that wasn't a surprising argument. In 1833 the Constitution didn't specifically say that blacks *were* U.S. citizens, and courts were sometimes asked to decide whether or not African Americans were entitled to full citizenship rights.

The jury listened as Andrew Judson finished his speech.

Now it was Mr. Ellsworth's turn to reply. Standing in front of the jury, Prudence's lawyer began to make his case.

Yes, the defense lawyer said, there was no doubt about it. Prudence had taught African-American children from out of state. She had broken the Connecticut Black Law. But that wasn't the issue. The real question was: Did the law Prudence broke violate the United States Constitution? The Constitution was the most important set of laws in America. All other laws had to agree with it. And, said Mr. Ellsworth, the law Prudence broke did not agree with the principles of the U.S. Constitution.

Carefully, he explained his points. The Connecticut Black Law said that African Americans from other states could not travel to Connecticut to be educated. But the Constitution said something different. It said that *all* U.S. citizens could travel freely from one state to another. And, said Mr. Ellsworth, *African Americans were U.S. citizens*. They were born in America like other citizens. They had fought for freedom in the American Revolution like other citizens. Besides, there was nothing in the Constitution that said black people were *not* full-fledged, one hundred percent American citizens.

Because the Connecticut Black Law violated the rights of African-American citizens, it violated the U.S. Constitution. It was a bad law, and breaking it was no crime.

Therefore, Mr. Ellsworth explained, Prudence was *not guilty*.

The lawyers were finished. Now it was up to the jury. The twelve men filed out. In the crowded courtroom Prudence and her friends waited. Everything was riding on the jury's verdict. Slowly the hours ticked by. People chatted or walked outside to get a breath of air. Men glanced impatiently at their watches. Then, finally, the door opened and the jurors filed back in. But when the judge asked if they'd reached a verdict, the foreman shook his head. The jury, he reported, couldn't decide. The judge asked them to reconsider. The spectators waited. Time passed. The door opened again, but the message was the same: no verdict. Again the judge ordered the jury to review the case. But when the jurors returned for the third time, there was still no decision.

Some members of the jury had believed the prosecution. Some had believed the defense. Seven jurors thought Prudence was guilty. Five were sure she was innocent. The jury was hopelessly split. Nothing had been decided. For Prudence the ordeal wasn't over. The case would have to be heard again, and a new trial was scheduled for December.

Chapter 12

More Trouble

There was no end to the insults. No end to the meanness. At least that's the way it must have seemed one August day when Prudence's housekeeper, Mariah Davis, hauled a bucket of water out of the school well. To her surprise, the pail was full of smelly brown muck. Someone had dumped a load of manure in Prudence's well. It was a dirty, disgusting trick. But Prudence couldn't afford to get upset over every outrage. Besides, at first, it didn't seem like a major problem. There were other places to get water. A neighbor who lived only a few steps away had a roadside well that he often let travelers use. But when a student tried to fetch a pail of water, the neighbor refused to let her have a single drop. That was unpleasant. Still, the situation wasn't alarming. There was another well nearby. But when Prudence asked to use it, the owner said no. None of the neighbors wanted to give her water, he explained.

That was serious. Water was a necessity. If the neighbors wouldn't help, Prudence would have to get along without them. Again she turned to her family; and, once again, Pardon hitched up his wagon. He hauled barrels of water to the school every day until his daughter managed to get a well in the school basement working.

Prudence told the girls "not to indulge in angry feelings towards [their] enemies." The girls, one student reported in an essay, tried to remember that they should "not return evil for evil." But it was probably hard not to be angry as the difficulties mounted.

When a student fell ill, Prudence called the nearest doctor, Andrew Harris. Grudgingly, Dr. Harris walked across the street and examined the sick girl, but he didn't plan to waste time on other black patients. "You need not send for me again," the doctor said as he left the house. "I shall not come if you do."

Worse yet, in September, Andrew Judson began to stir up trouble.

The school was in his way. Despite all his efforts, the

Dr. Andrew Harris's house, which still stands across the street from the Crandall school. Neither Dr. Harris nor his neighbor, Andrew Judson, wanted a school for black girls near their expensive homes.

stubborn teacher and her black pupils were still sitting in the big white house in the middle of town. Judson couldn't walk out the front door of his own fancy mansion without seeing Miss Crandall's academy across the street, and he wanted the place closed down. Of course, the school would have to shut if Prudence was declared guilty at her new trial in December, but Andrew Judson didn't want to wait that long. With the help of a few well-placed friends, he managed to get the process moving.

The results were instantaneous.

On September 26 the Canterbury sheriff tried to arrest Prudence again. This time, however, friends paid her bail before the town authorities could haul her off to prison.

One day later, on September 27, there was another unpleasant surprise. The date of Prudence's new trial had been moved. Instead of being held in December as originally planned, it was scheduled to take place in six days. No one was ready. Samuel May was out of town. Prudence's chief lawyer, Mr. Ellsworth, wasn't available. His two colleagues had almost no time to prepare. Prudence barely had time to gather her thoughts before the court session opened at nine A.M. on October 3, 1833.

For those who had watched the first trial, it was a little like seeing a rerun. Once again Prudence sat in the courtroom, listening to the arguments, scanning the jury box, and wondering what the jurors were thinking. Again, the prosecution lawyers argued that Prudence had broken the Connecticut Black Law by teaching African-American girls. And again the defense argued that breaking the Connecticut law didn't matter because blacks were U.S. citizens and the Black Law violated the rights given to African-American citizens by the U.S. Constitution.

The arguments were the same. But the jury was different. So was the judge. Presiding judge David Daggett was a well-dressed man with a lordly manner and an actor's booming voice. Two years earlier, he had helped stop abolitionists from opening a school for African-American men in New Haven. He didn't think much of black people, and he wasn't shy about saying so.

Miss Crandall's lawyers were dead wrong, Judge Daggett told the jury. The Connecticut Black Law did not violate the rights given to black citizens by the U.S. Constitution. It couldn't do that because blacks *were not* American citizens. They were a "degraded caste, of inferior rank and condition in society," Daggett said. They had no constitutional rights, and the U.S. Constitution had nothing to do with the Crandall case.

The jury, he said, had to deal with just one single fact: Prudence Crandall had broken a Connecticut state law.

The twelve jurors listened carefully and left the room. When they returned, the verdict was "guilty."

But Prudence's lawyers weren't going to settle for that. Before Judge Daggett could sentence Prudence to fines or imprisonment, they filed an appeal asking the Supreme Court of Errors—the highest, most powerful court in Connecticut—to review the case and decide if the guilty verdict was correct. That process would take months. In the meantime, however, Prudence was free. The school was open. More students were enrolling. Andrew Judson and the Canterbury townsfolk hadn't won yet.

Chapter 13

Fire!

The skies were gray, and the cold November wind whipped around the corners of the big white schoolhouse. Logs burned in the fireplaces, and sometimes at night the girls sat around the flames chatting. For a change, there were even happy things to chat about.

First, there was the new man who'd been calling on Miss Crandall. He was a tall man, a Baptist minister, named Calvin Philleo. Of course, he was old—at least forty-six. His wife was dead, and the Reverend Philleo was taking care of a teenage daughter and a twelve-year-old son. Some of the girls had seen him at Prudence's trial, sitting with the spectators in the courtroom, wearing a bright blue necktie. Others had seen him when he called at the house. He wasn't exactly handsome, but he did have a fine, rich, musical voice.

Of course, Prudence didn't discuss the Reverend Philleo with the girls, but that wasn't likely to stop them from wondering about a romance. In any case, love was in the air. Mariah Davis, Prudence's housekeeper, and her friend, student Sarah Harris, were both going to be married at the end of November in a double wedding, and the whole school was invited to the ceremony. Prudence's sister, Almira, was making Mariah's wedding dress, and the girls were all busy helping Sarah and Mariah get ready.

A fireplace in the Crandall house today. In Prudence's time, when fires were the only source of heat, students and teachers probably clustered around the hearth while studying or chatting.

After a Thanksgiving Day party, the two brides said their vows. Then it was time for goodbyes. Sarah and her new husband, George Fayerweather, were going to live in Rhode Island, where George had a blacksmith business. Mariah and her husband, Charles Harris, settled down in Canterbury so that Mariah could keep working at the school.

Christmas came. The holidays passed, and when the

church bells rang in the new year Prudence must have hoped that 1834 would be better than 1833 had been.

Of course, none of her big problems had been solved. The Supreme Court of Errors still hadn't decided whether to let the guilty verdict against her stand. The Canterbury townsfolk still went out of their way to be unpleasant. It was more of the same, and there was no point in dwelling on it. The women at Miss Crandall's school had better things to do. There were lessons to learn, letters to write, chores to do, and visitors to entertain.

On January 28, Prudence interrupted her morning schedule to welcome Frederick Olney, an African-American handyman who helped William Lloyd Garrison distribute the *Liberator*. Olney had stopped by to deliver some bundles and say hello to his friends Mariah and Charles Harris. But first Prudence sat him down in front of a cozy fire in a downstairs parlor. While Olney was warming himself, he noticed that the clock on the mantel wasn't ticking steadily. He mentioned it to Prudence, who admitted she hadn't even noticed the irregular tick. Still, the clock bothered Olney, and the ticking was on his mind when he went off to see Mariah and her husband. After lunch, determined to fix the annoying clock, Olney went back to the parlor.

Students wandered in and out while he fiddled with the

mechanism. The adjustment took a bit of doing, and he was working on it when Amy Fenner, one of the girls, said she saw smoke.

Alarmed, Olney checked the room. Except for the blaze in the fireplace, he couldn't see anything. The carpet wasn't on fire. Neither were the evergreen garlands on the wall. But the room was filling with smoke. "What does this mean?" Amy gasped as she pointed to wisps of smoke issuing from a corner. Instantly, Olney pressed his ear against the wall. Flames were roaring behind the panels. He yelled for an ax. Then he raced through the door and outside. There, just above one of the first-floor windows, a little flame

Clock on the mantel of a room the Crandall house today. The clock Frederick Olney tried to fix on the day of the fire may have looked like this.

sparked. Olney dashed a tub of water against the wall, grabbed an ax from Charles Harris, and began chopping at the side of the house.

Somebody yelled that the school was on fire. The fire bell clanged. Men from all over Canterbury ran toward the house. A crowd gathered. The burning school was a threat to every building in town, and Prudence's neighbors battled their way through the smoke, ripped up the parlor wall with their axes, and managed to stop the flames.

The fire was out. The house was safe. Prudence and the girls were unharmed. But people in Canterbury began to wonder how the blaze had started. Some said that Prudence had set it herself to get sympathy. Others disagreed, but people wanted to blame someone. Rumors spread. When a few townspeople heard that Olney had been near the spot where the fire started, suspicion focused on him. It was easy for people in Canterbury to blame a black man, and readers of the *Unionist,* the paper that Arthur Tappan had founded, suddenly learned that Olney had been arrested for "feloniously, voluntarily, maliciously, and willfully set[ting] fire to the dwelling house of Miss Prudence Crandall."

Prudence knew he was innocent. Fair-minded people realized that Olney was actually a hero. But everyone from the fire insurance investigators to Prudence believed that someone had deliberately started the fire. Some unknown person had hated the Crandall school enough to burn down the house with Prudence and about twenty young women inside.

Corner of a room in the Crandall house as it might have looked in Prudence's day. The wooden stand bearing the washbowl and pitcher marks the corner of the house where the fire started in 1834.

As usual, Prudence consulted the Reverend May. Together, they discussed whether or not it was safe to keep the school open. Despite the danger, they decided that Prudence could hold out. But both of them knew the situation had changed. The fire was more than an insult or a nasty trick. It was a vicious attack. Someone had wanted to hurt Prudence and her students, and no one knew whether—or when—that person would try again.

Chapter 14

"The Choicest Blessing"

THE YEAR 1834 hadn't begun well, but by spring things were looking up. Helen Benson noticed that Prudence was looking "unusually handsome," and the reason was clear. She was in love. Calvin Philleo, the tall Baptist minister, had asked her to marry him. After thinking it over, Prudence had said yes.

At thirty-one, Prudence was at least ten years past the age when most girls married in the 1800s. Although she had built a fine teaching career in her twenties, Prudence also wanted other things. "I wish I had a lover/ I'm longing to be loved," she wrote in a poem once. Now, at last, it seemed she had met someone who could share her joys and help shoulder her troubles. Besides, Calvin seemed particularly understanding. At a time when few middle-class husbands allowed their wives to work, he was willing to let the famous Miss Crandall continue to run her school. It was no wonder that Prudence told Helen Benson that he was the "choicest blessing."

But that wasn't all. In the spring of 1834 good news was coming in floods. First, there was word that both newlyweds, Sarah and Mariah, were pregnant. Then, on a rainy March day, a Connecticut jury found that Frederick Olney was not guilty of setting the Crandall school on fire.

Of course, Prudence and her friends had always known that Olney was innocent. They knew it was his quick thinking that had saved the school. Still, they had worried, knowing that Olney might have been convicted simply because his skin was black. That hadn't happened, and Helen Benson noticed that the sun came out from behind the rain clouds just as the jury's verdict was announced.

At last the tide seemed to be turning. Instead of insults and criticism, gifts and encouraging letters poured in. A group of ladies in Edinburgh, Scotland, sent a large, expensive Bible "to Miss Crandall . . . as a mark of the respect with which they regard the Christian courage of her conduct toward their colored Sisters in the United States." The Glasgow Emancipation Society presented Prudence with a

Helen Benson Garrison, William Lloyd Garrison's wife and one of Prudence's best friends.

piece of silver to show their admiration of her "praiseworthy and heroic conduct in the cause of education among the colored females of the United States." Others sent china plates, books, pincushions, and pen wipers. A few admirers praised Miss Crandall in bad but heartfelt poetry. There was even a letter from William Lloyd Garrison telling Prudence that the New England Anti-Slavery Society wanted her to come to Boston to have her portrait painted by Francis Alexander, a well-known artist.

Garrison was in Boston to greet her, and crowds of people turned out to see the heroine of Canterbury. In between parties and receptions, Prudence posed for the artist in a fashionable dress. Garrison came by the studio to keep her company, but instead of paying attention to Prudence, he kept staring at a portrait Alexander had painted of a girl who looked just like his fiancée, Helen Benson—one of Prudence's closest friends.

After all those weary months, encouragement seemed to be coming from every direction. In 1834, antislavery societies sprang up in towns around Canterbury. The *Boston Press* declared, "If Miss Crandall has a right to receive white scholars from other states, she has an equal right to receive colored ones." Even more gratifying was the news that Prudence had apparently inspired other teachers. New schools for African-American girls opened in Boston and Philadelphia, and the *Liberator* carried ads for "a private school for colored youth" and "an evening school for people of color" in Boston. Then, in the middle of April, came the icing on the cake: Andrew Judson was defeated when he ran for reelection to the Connecticut legislature. Clearly, there were some people in the state who didn't agree with the way Judson and the Canterbury townsfolk had treated Prudence and her African-American students.

Of course, there were still problems. William Burleigh, Prudence's assistant teacher at the Crandall school, was pelted with rotten eggs as he walked home one night; and Canterbury vandals killed a cat, cut its throat, and hung the corpse on Prudence's gate. Almost as disturbing were the nasty rumors about Prudence's fiancé, Calvin Philleo. Gossip said he'd been fired from one Connecticut church for acting like a tyrant. A clergyman in another parish accused

The "Zion" school for black children in Charleston, South Carolina, in 1866. After the Civil War, many other teachers—following Prudence's example—opened schools for African Americans.

him of being a little too friendly with married women in the congregation. Some said he was so eager to have a mother for his young children that he'd marry any female on two feet. In fact, they said, he'd actually advertised for a wife.

Prudence's friends heard the rumors and begged her to be careful. They wanted her to be happy, but they didn't trust Calvin Philleo. Helen Benson was suspicious when

Calvin refused to look her in the eye. Dr. Roland Green, another of Prudence's abolitionist friends, thought the minister was "very disagreeable, and took a very great dislike to him." Even Prudence was a little worried when Calvin completely ignored her for weeks on end. But, she couldn't believe the ugly rumors about him. In a letter to her fiancé, William Lloyd Garrison, Helen Benson sadly explained that Prudence thought Calvin was an "almost perfect being." No one could tell her otherwise. The trouble was, said Helen, Calvin "could make Prudence believe black was white if he chose."

June passed. New England celebrated the Fourth of July. Then, suddenly, there was terrible news. Race riots had broken out in New York City. People who hated abolitionists had assaulted members of an antislavery society, and the violence had spun out of control. An angry mob had attacked African Americans on the streets. It had also damaged black homes, black churches, and a black school. Rioters burst into the home of Arthur Tappan's abolitionist brother, dragged his furniture into the street, and set it on fire. A day later armed men had to drive the mob away from Arthur Tappan's store. For Prudence, it was a relief to know that neither of the Tappan brothers had been hurt. But the riot was a terrifying reminder of just how much some Americans despised black people and those who stood up for African-American rights.

It was a reminder Prudence could have done without. She already had plenty of worries. The Supreme Court of Errors was ready to hear her case, and on July 26, 1834, Andrew Judson and Prudence's lawyer, William Ellsworth, presented their arguments to a panel of judges in the Brooklyn courthouse. This time there were no witnesses and no testimony. The only issue was whether or not the guilty verdict that had been handed down against Prudence at her second trial had been reached in a fair and correct manner.

Once again, William Ellsworth told the court that Miss Crandall was innocent. The law she broke violated the United States Constitution, he argued, because it denied African-American citizens the basic rights of all U.S. citizens.

Now it was Andrew Judson's turn. Once again the Canterbury lawyer told the court that Prudence Crandall was guilty. The law she broke did not violate the U.S. Constitution, he said, because the Constitution protected only American citizens, and blacks did not have any citizenship rights. Besides, Judson added, "America belongs to a race of white men."

The judges listened and considered the arguments. A few

Race riots—like the New York riot that endangered the Tappan brothers—were common in the 1830s, and white mobs often attacked African Americans and abolitionists on the streets of northern cities. Here, a mob burns the warehouse of the Illinois abolitionist Elijah Lovejoy in 1837. Lovejoy himself was murdered as he tried to escape.

days later they announced their decision: Prudence Crandall was not guilty.

She couldn't be fined for breaking the Black Law. She couldn't be put in jail. It was a victory for Prudence. Yet it wasn't a huge triumph. The trouble was, the judges had ignored the principal issues in the case. They had not decided whether the Connecticut Black Law violated the principles of the U.S. Constitution, and they had not decided whether

African Americans were really citizens of the United States. The judges had simply canceled the guilty verdict because of a tiny, technical legal mistake in the wording of the original arrest warrant.

Andrew Judson and the Canterbury townsfolk were furious. All their attempts to stop Prudence legally had failed.

Abolitionists were disappointed. They had hoped that the court would decide that African Americans were truly U.S. citizens and order the state of Connecticut to get rid of the Black Law once and for all.

No one was satisfied. Still, the decision meant that Prudence could get on with her life, and there was one thing at the top of her agenda. On August 12, 1834, she married Calvin Philleo. A Canterbury minister refused to perform the ceremony, so the couple said their vows in a Brooklyn church. Then they left on a honeymoon trip to Boston and Philadelphia.

Prudence was radiant, but her friends were afraid the marriage was a huge mistake. When William Lloyd Garrison met the bride and groom in Boston, he couldn't bring himself to say congratulations. Instead, he told his fiancée, Helen Benson, that he had politely wished the couple "much happiness."

Prudence, however, didn't seem concerned about her

friends' misgivings. After the wedding trip was over, she settled Calvin, his daughter, and his young son in her Canterbury house and went back to work. Her legal problems had been resolved. Her school was famous. She had a new family to love, and the future was looking bright.

Prudence Crandall as she looked shortly before her marriage. In a letter William Lloyd Garrison told his fiancée, "I am happy to say that the artist has been very successful in taking the portrait of Miss Crandall; but the story of her persecution will outlive the canvas."

Chapter 15

"For Sale"

THE GOOD NEWS KEPT coming. On September 4, Samuel May married a very happy William Lloyd Garrison to the dark-haired Helen Benson. Five days later, in Rhode Island, Sarah Harris Fayerweather gave birth to a little girl she named Prudence Crandall Fayerweather.

At the school, Prudence's new stepson and stepdaughter settled into their new home. Prudence taught. Calvin preached at a nearby Baptist church. The girls concentrated on their lessons. On September 9, the day Sarah had her baby, everything seemed to be going smoothly. After a day of work and study, the family and students had dinner, said good night, turned out the lights, and went to bed. By midnight the house was quiet. The residents were fast asleep when a bloodcurdling shriek ripped through the darkness. Screaming men pounded the school doors, walls, and windows with clubs and iron bars. Glass shattered. Wood splintered. Walls shook. Men burst through the door and stormed through the ground floor, smashing furniture and hurling it to the floor. Then it was quiet.

When the sun came up, Prudence surveyed the damage. No one was hurt, but five window frames had been ripped to pieces. Glass from ninety shattered windowpanes crunched underfoot, and bits of broken furniture littered the floor. The students were terrified, and one frightened girl was coughing up blood.

Prudence was devastated. She'd endured prison, legal trials, a fire, a boycott, and months of insults, but this was too much. She couldn't face her students. It was William Burleigh, Prudence's assistant teacher, who told the frightened girls that classes had been canceled for the day. Then he left the house and headed for Brooklyn, to carry the news to Samuel May.

That afternoon the two men returned to Canterbury. Inside the school, a horrified May stared at the wreckage. The front rooms were unusable; the students, unnerved. After the fire, May had urged Prudence not to give in. Now, as he looked at the smashed windows and broken furniture, the minister knew the situation was hopeless. There was no point in making repairs. The Canterbury vandals would only strike again. This time the school had been damaged. Next time someone might be seriously hurt.

As the bright September sun streamed in through the shattered windows, Prudence and May discussed the problem. There were few alternatives, and finally Prudence asked her good friend to do her one last favor.

With a heavy heart, May called the girls together and told them it was time to pack their bags. There was no choice, he said. The school would have to close. It was the only sensible course, but the sad, bitter words "almost blistered [May's] lips" as he spoke. "I felt ashamed of Canterbury . . . ashamed of my country, ashamed of my color," the minister later wrote.

In an essay, one of the students described how the girls said their tearful goodbyes. Despite the abuse, despite the insults and the fears, the pupils cherished memories of their teacher's kindness. For the girls, the student said, the Crandall school had been a "place of communion with Heaven."

There was only one thing left to do. On September 11, Calvin placed an ad in the *Liberator*.

"For sale," it said, "the house in Canterbury occupied by . . . Prudence Crandall."

By November 15 the big white house had been sold and the family had moved in with Prudence's parents. A few months later, Calvin decided to move his wife and children to a small farm he owned in upstate New York. The Canterbury townsfolk probably were not sorry to see them go.

On a spring day in 1835, barely two years after she'd welcomed her first black pupils, Prudence Crandall Philleo boarded the stagecoach that would take her and her family out of Canterbury, Connecticut.

As the horses jogged down the familiar roads, Prudence's thoughts may have drifted back over all that had happened since she'd first met Sarah Harris. Since then she'd lost her school. She'd lost her home. Her plans to educate young black women had collapsed. Of course, she had tried to do something important. She had faced trouble and fought a good fight. But did any of that really matter? As the coach sped down the long road leading out of Canterbury, Prudence probably believed her enemies had won.

Chapter 16

"Deep Convictions of Right"

FIFTY YEARS PASSED. Fourteen new states were admitted to the Union. Sixteen different presidents had sat in the White House. For four long, bloody years, between 1861 and 1865, the Civil War had torn at the heart of the nation. In 1865 slavery was abolished. Three years later, the Fourteenth Amendment, which stated that blacks were U.S. citizens, was added to the U.S. Constitution. Then, in 1869, another amendment, the fifteenth, gave African Americans the right to vote. Little by little the country changed. Railroad men laid a shining ribbon of track across the continent, from the Atlantic Ocean to the blue Pacific. Elias Howe made the first sewing machine. Thomas Edison invented the electric light, and in 1886 a newspaper reporter named George Thayer decided to travel from Hartford, Connecticut, to San Francisco on a newfangled machine called a bicycle. Along the way, he planned to interview interesting people. One of them was Prudence Crandall.

A print drawn by the artist G. F. Kahl showing (*center*) men celebrating the passage of the Fifteenth Amendment to the Constitution, which gave African Americans the right to vote. The pictures on the sides show that African Americans believed that proper schooling and good jobs were an important part of citizenship.

He found her in Kansas, living in a little prairie town called Elk Falls. She was eighty-four—a thin, stooped, almost toothless woman in a shabby black cotton dress. Her short gray hair was cropped off just below the ears, and two bright blue eyes sparkled in her wrinkled face.

"I am glad to see anyone from good old Connecticut," she told Thayer in a pleasant voice. "You must be hungry, coming so far."

Picture from the book George Thayer wrote about his travels, showing Thayer with the bicycle he rode on his trip to visit Prudence.

She sat him down by the fire and stuffed him full of ham, potatoes, bread and butter, ginger-snaps, tea, and apple pie. Then, when Thayer had swallowed the last mouthful, the old lady pulled up a rocking chair by his side and began to talk about her adventures.

A lot had happened since she'd ridden away from Canterbury on that spring day more than fifty years ago.

Her mother, father, brothers, and sister had died. Her own life had been difficult, and her marriage had been a disaster.

Soon after the wedding, Calvin began to show signs of mental illness. He had seizures and lost his memory. Sometimes he behaved like a helpless child. At other times he bullied his family, ordered Prudence around, refused to let her read certain books, and frittered away his small income on crazy deals and investments. Prudence had no time to work with abolitionists or teach black children. She took care of her husband. She brought up Calvin's son. She tended his sickly daughter until the girl died, but by 1842 Prudence had reached the end of her patience.

Prudence Crandall at age seventy-one.

She was forty years old, and she wanted to start a new life. Her stepchildren no longer needed her care. Her husband was intolerable and probably demented. Divorce was expensive and difficult. Divorce laws favored men, and in the 1800s most people thought dissolving a marriage was sinful and scandalous. For Prudence, there was only one way to escape. She packed a bag, left her husband, and headed out to Illinois to set up a farm on some land her family owned. With only her thirteen-year-old nephew to help, Prudence sowed oats and put up fences. She piled dung on potato plants to keep them from freezing, and she started to build a house.

The farm did well. Calvin didn't. He needed care, and

Prudence felt she had to help. After only two years in Illinois, she traveled back to the East Coast to nurse her husband.

To make a living, Prudence taught reading classes for black adults, many of whom had once been slaves. Teaching however, didn't pay the bills, and Prudence was soon down to her last few dollars. Luckily, her nephew, Obediah, had kept up the farm in Illinois, and Prudence knew she was welcome there. She invited Calvin to go west. When he couldn't make up his mind, she hopped on a canal boat and headed back to Illinois without him.

Prudence Crandall's little house on the Kansas prairie near Elk Falls. Reproduction of a sketch in the *Kansas City Journal,* March 28, 1886.

For the next few years Prudence ran a prairie school and continued to work for abolition. As the Union and Confederate armies clashed on the batttlefield, neighbors saw her standing in the street, dressed in trousers and an overcoat, passing out antislavery pamphlets.

But no matter where Prudence went or what she did, there was always Calvin. He was useless, ornery, and undoubtedly insane, but still, when he came west and needed help—once again—Prudence took him in. Instead of being grateful, Calvin upset the household. He abused animals, called his wife "old squash-head," drove Prudence crazy with his endless prayers, and finally died on January 5, 1874.

It was time for a fresh start, and when Prudence's brother Hezekiah came west, she settled down with him on some land near Elk Falls, Kansas.

Prudence liked Kansas. The farm prospered and life was good. Then, in the bitter winter of 1881, Hezekiah suddenly died of pnemonia. Prudence grieved and went on.

While a young man took care of the farm chores, seventy-eight-year-old Prudence began to work for her favorite causes. When former slaves flooded into Kansas after the Civil War to escape harsh treatment in the South, she supported efforts to help these struggling African Americans. In Elk Falls, Prudence organized temperance festivals to teach children about the dangers of drinking alcohol. She campaigned for women's rights and world peace. "I am earnestly engaged in . . . every reform for the good of the human race," Prudence told a reporter from the *Topeka Daily Capital*. Besides, she added, "I hope to live long enough to see a college built on this farm into which can be admitted all classes of the human family without regard to sex or color."

Her mind was sharp. Her days were long and busy. She had no money. Her home was a little rundown, book-filled shack on the Kansas prairie, almost two miles from her nearest neighbor. But if Prudence had regrets, she didn't talk about them. The past was past. She seemed to be looking toward the future. Certainly, in 1885, at the age of eighty-three, the very last thing she probably expected was a message from Canterbury, Connecticut.

Fifty years after her school had closed, the town had decided to apologize.

One hundred and twelve Canterbury citizens had signed a petition asking the Connecticut state legislature to clear Prudence's name and repay her for the financial losses she had suffered when her school was forced to close.

Times had changed. Canterbury had learned a lesson, and many Connecticut residents were ashamed of the way they had treated Prudence and her African-American students.

Philip Pearl, one of the authors of the infamous Black Law that Prudence had broken, told a friend that he could "weep tears of blood" for his part in the attack on Miss Crandall and her school. The Black Law, he confessed, was "utterly abominable."

Others shared his feelings. In 1838 the Connecticut legislature struck down the Black Law and made it possible for African-American students from all over the United States to go to school in Connecticut.

In the years between 1838 and the start of the Civil War in 1861, antislavery societies flourished in Connecticut, and the state became an important stop on the Underground Railroad. In Windham County, where people had once hurled rotten eggs at Prudence's students, thirteen agents regularly helped runaway slaves to freedom. Later, in 1868, Connecticut became one of the first states to ratify (approve) the Fourteenth Amendment to the Constitution that officially made African Americans full-fledged citizens of the United States.

Attitudes toward blacks had altered, but they hadn't changed completely.

In 1885, when the Canterbury townsfolk presented their petition, the Connecticut legislature didn't rush to send money or apologies to Prudence. Some lawmakers claimed

Mark Twain, the famous American author, who supported efforts to help Prudence in the 1880s. In a thank-you note, Prudence asked Twain to send her some of his books and a photo of himself. Twain wrote back to say he'd be happy to oblige.

they didn't feel obligated to do anything for Miss Crandall because she had once broken a Connecticut state law. But others had an entirely different view.

At a meeting of the legislature, Senator John W. Marvin begged his fellow Connecticut lawmakers to help Prudence. "Our heroine still lives," Marvin said. "She can know and appreciate our acts in her behalf. . . . If this general assembly shall even in part right this great wrong she will go down to her grave, not only in peace but with gratitude for her native state."

Marvin wasn't alone, and, as the weeks went by, support mounted. The son of the Canterbury sheriff who had once arrested Prudence campaigned for her. One of Andrew Judson's relatives asked the legislature to help Prudence. Mark Twain, the famous author of *The Adventures of Tom Sawyer* and *The Adventures of Huckleberry Finn,* tried to persuade well-wishers to buy back Prudence's original Canterbury house so that she would always have a home to live in. Even newspapers took her side. One, the *Springfield (Mass.) Republican,* said bluntly, "She was right in teaching Negro children."

Prudence herself had mixed emotions. She didn't want people to feel sorry for her, but she did feel the state of Connecticut owed her some compensation for her financial losses and suffering. When a reporter from the *Topeka Daily Capital* asked how she felt, Prudence explained matters simply. "I do not consider I am an object of charity," she said, "but I do ask the Connecticut legislature to pay me a little part of a just debt that I feel they are in duty bound to pay."

Finally, on April 2, 1886, Prudence received a telegram. It said the legislature had voted to grant her a pension of $400 a year until her death. When reporter George Thayer asked how she felt about that, Prudence replied, "If the people of Connecticut only knew how happy I am . . . it would make them happy too."

With the pension money, Prudence bought a decent two-story house in Elk Falls. She was eighty-four years old. She had plenty of energy, and she wanted to work. Neighbors soon got used to seeing a bent old lady dressed in black marching down the street with a white cheesecloth peace flag slung over her shoulder. It was Prudence, on her way to lecture on the evils of war or the importance of women's rights in a schoolhouse or meeting hall.

Prudence was famous, but it didn't change the way she lived. At eighty-five she was still a fighter. Money didn't interest her. New things did. She ate up books. She even read about Charles Darwin's controversial new theory that said all creatures, including humans, had gradually evolved from primitive one-celled animals.

Still, age began to take its toll. At eighty-six, Prudence began to have trouble breathing. Something seemed to be wrong with her lungs, but she didn't want to give in to it. "Mind has great power over matter and I think I can drive away the disease," she said. But this time willpower wasn't enough. In January 1890 Prudence knew she was dying. When her friend the Reverend McKesson asked what he should preach in her funeral sermon, the old lady answered

Prudence Crandall's gravestone, Elk Falls, Kansas. The inscription reads:

CRANDALL
PRUDENCE CRANDALL PHILLEO
OF CANTERBURY, CONN.
SEPTEMBER 3, 1803 TO JANUARY 28, 1890

simply, "Preach the truth." Later she added, "I am no more afraid to die than I am to live." There was little more to say. A few days later, on the morning of January 28, Prudence quietly passed away.

They buried her in the Elk Falls cemetery, and the Reverend McKesson spoke at her grave. She was a great woman, he said. "She had deep convictions of right . . . [and] neither death, life, angels, principalities . . . nor any other creatures could keep her from following her convictions."

Epilogue

"There's a better day a coming
Oh, Glory, Hallelujah!"
—African-American spiritual

PRUDENCE DIED BUT WAS NOT FORGOTTEN. Today, her home in Canterbury has been turned into a museum. She has been named Connecticut's state female hero.* Her struggle has had an impact on one of the most important Supreme Court cases in U.S. history, and others have continued her fight to educate African Americans.

After the Civil War, many teachers—including some of Prudence's former students—opened schools for blacks, and the number of African Americans who could read and write increased rapidly. Unfortunately, southern states soon passed segregation laws that made it illegal for whites and blacks to attend the same schools. While white southern children went to well-built, well-funded modern schools,

* Connecticut's male hero is Revolutionary War soldier Nathan Hale.

Attorney Thurgood Marshall standing on the steps of the U.S. Supreme Court building, the site of his battle to overturn school segregation laws.

African-American students in southern states often did their lessons in tumble-down wooden shacks without proper heat, supplies, or running water. Some states did not even provide high schools for black children.

To fight these laws, African Americans turned to the courts. At first they made little headway. Then, in the early 1950s, in a case known as *Brown v. Board of Education of Topeka,* attorney Thurgood Marshall asked the U.S. Supreme Court to overturn state laws requiring the separation of black and white children in public schools. In his presentation to the court, Marshall cited many arguments—including some dealing with human equality and equal laws that were first presented at Prudence Crandall's trial by her attorney, William Ellsworth.

Little Rock, Arkansas, September 4, 1957. Arkansas National Guardsmen, called out by the state governor to stop school desegregation, prevent fifteen-year-old Elizabeth Eckford from entering all white Central High School.

On May 17, 1954, Marshall was victorious, and the U.S. Supreme Court banned racial discrimination in American public schools. At first, however, some southerners tried to resist the order. In Little Rock, Arkansas, 125 years after Canterbury citizens threw stones at Prudence's pupils, President Eisenhower had to order U.S. troops to protect black students who tried to attend a formerly all white high school from an angry white mob.

Slowly segregation disappeared in southern schools, but other racial and educational problems remained.

Although segregation laws were never passed in northern states, prejudice against African Americans was strong, and after the Civil War blacks were often denied entry to many northern schools on account of race. In the early 1960s, roughly ten years after Thurgood Marshall's great victory in the Supreme Court, there were still so few good educational opportunities for African Americans nationwide that President Kennedy declared, "The Negro baby born in America today—regardless of the section or state in which he is born—has about one-half as much chance of completing high school as a white baby born in the same place on the same day—one-third as much chance of completing college—one-third as much chance of becoming a professional man."

Little Rock, Arkansas, 1957. U. S. soldiers called out by President Eisenhower to protect black students trying to attend previously all white schools give an African-American student and his bike a safe ride to class.

In the 1960s, as the result of the civil rights movement, educational opportunities for blacks increased as racial barriers began to fall. In 1965, President Johnson gave a boost to African-American education by starting an affirmative

June, 2000. White and African-American second-graders eat lunch together at a public school in Mississippi.

action policy that ordered schools receiving money from the federal government to make a special effort to admit minority students. A few years later, the Supreme Court ruled that public schools in the North and South that were still segregated because blacks and whites lived in different neighborhoods could be integrated by busing.

Today, American schools are open to students of all races. Laws prevent the kind of prejudice that Prudence Crandall's students encountered, and many African Americans—in both the North and the South—now have professional jobs and send their children to good schools. But despite these gains, many American blacks are still likely to receive less education and go to poorer schools than whites. Although more African-American students have entered college than ever before, only 11 percent of all U.S. college students are black. That is not enough. If Prudence were alive today, she would probably still be fighting to ensure that all African-American children receive a good education.

Appendix

Part I: The Students

THE AFRICAN-AMERICAN GIRLS, aged roughly nine to nineteen, who attended the Crandall school were as courageous as their teacher. Although no complete school roster exists, evidence suggests that there were probably about twenty pupils. Very little is known about most of these young women. In some cases, even their exact names are in doubt, but researchers have uncovered a few facts about the pupils listed alphabetically below.

Henrietta Bolt, a student from New York, testified about the school fire at Frederick Olney's trial.

Elizabeth D. Bustill came from Philadelphia and was the daughter of a teacher who also helped fugitive slaves.

M. E. Carter, Jeruska Congdon, and **Theodosia DeGrasse** came from New York.

Sarah Harris Fayerweather, Prudence's first black pupil, was the daughter of a respectable Connecticut farmer. After her marriage to blacksmith George Fayerweather, Sarah moved to Rhode Island. There, the Fayerweather home became a center of abolitionist activity, and Sarah provided food, clothing, medicine, and shelter to many slaves escaping from the South via the Underground Railroad. She corresponded with Prudence throughout her life, and two of her children became teachers. After her death in 1879, a dormitory at the University of Rhode Island was named after her.

Amy Fenner was the student who first noticed the fire. She testified at Frederick Olney's trial.

Polly Freeman came from New York.

Eliza Glasko came from Griswold, Connecticut. Her father, Isaac, a blacksmith, ran a large business that employed more than thirty people. He made tools for farmers and carpenters and specialized in producing harpoons and other instruments for the whaling industry. Eliza was called as a witness at Prudence's trial.

Ann Eliza Hammond and **Sarah Lloyd Hammond,** sisters, became Prudence's students at the ages of seventeen and nine, respectively. The girls, who originally lived in Providence, Rhode Island, lost their father at an early age and were brought up by their mother. Ann Eliza was Prudence's first out-of-state student and was threatened with whipping by the Canterbury village authorities.

Mary Harris (Sarah Harris Fayerweather's younger sister) became a teacher after leaving Prudence's school. Both she and her husband, Pelluman Williams, taught African-American students in Greensburg, Louisiana, after the Civil War. Her oldest son also became a teacher and headmaster in a New Orleans school.

Elizabeth Henly and **J. K. Johnson** came from Pennsylvania.

Harriet Rosetta Lamson, the adopted daughter of the Reverend Simeon Jocelyn (a white abolitionist minister), became Prudence's student at the age of fifteen. Since Jocelyn could not afford to pay her full tuition, Harriet did some housework at the school to pay her way. After leaving the Crandall school, Harriet taught Jocelyn's children and worked to ban the drinking of alcohol. She died at the age of eighteen.

G. C. Marshall came from New York.

Ann Peterson, a student from New York, was threatened with whipping by the Canterbury village authorities. She was called to testify at Prudence's trial.

Mariah Robinson, a student from Rhode Island, gave evidence about the fire at Frederick Olney's trial.

Elizabeth N. Smith was taught by Quaker tutors before she attended the Crandall school. She became a teacher and eventually rose to be principal of a school in her hometown, Providence, Rhode Island.

Catherine Ann Weldon, a student from New York, was called to testify at Prudence's trial.

Amilia Elizabeth Wilder (or Wiles), a student from New York, was asked to appear at Prudence's trial, but could not attend because she had to return home to care for her sick mother.

Julia Williams was born in Charleston, South Carolina, and moved to Boston when she was very young. After leaving the Crandall school, she continued to study at the Noyes Academy in Canaan, New Hampshire, until it was destroyed by an armed white mob in 1835. Julia finished her education at the Oneida Institute in New York and taught at an elementary school in Boston. In 1837 she was chosen as a delegate to the Annual Women's Anti-Slavery Convention in New York City. Three years later she married Henry Highland Garnet, a brilliant speaker who was an important figure in the African-American abolitionist movement. After their marriage, Julia and her husband worked as missionaries in the British West Indies. Julia died in 1870 at the age of fifty-nine; her husband was named U.S. ambassador to Liberia in 1881.

Part II: Friends and Enemies

IN THE YEARS THAT FOLLOWED the closure of Prudence's school, many of her associates continued to be involved in the struggle for equal rights and African-American education. Here, in brief, are their stories.

William Ellsworth: After defending Prudence, Ellsworth retired from the U.S. Congress. He became governor of Connecticut in 1838 and was later appointed associate justice of the Supreme Court of Connecticut. Although Ellsworth died in 1868, some of the arguments he presented at Prudence's trial helped attorney Thurgood Marshall convince the U.S. Supreme Court to ban racial segregation in all American public schools in 1954.

William Lloyd Garrison: Despite being reviled, threatened, and even dragged through the streets at the end of a rope by an angry proslavery mob, Garrison continued to publish the *Liberator* and fight for abolition. Because he hated violence and hoped to end slavery without bloodshed, he refused to support the Civil War until President Lincoln freed slaves in the Confederate states by issuing the Emancipation Proclamation in 1863. Garrison published the last issue of the *Liberator* on December 29, 1865, a few days after ratification of the Thirteenth Amendment to the Constitution officially abolished slavery in the United States. After the war, Garrison worked to educate former slaves. He also supported the struggle to give women the right to vote, campaigned for rights for Native Americans, and objected to discrimination against Chinese immigrants. He corresponded with Prudence in later years and died on May 24, 1879.

Andrew Judson: After serving briefly in the U.S. Congress, Judson was appointed a U.S. Circuit Court judge by President Andrew Jackson and surprised many of his abolitionist critics by making an important court decision in favor of blacks. In 1839, when a group of illegally imported African slaves escaped from their Cuban masters and landed on American shores, Judge Judson was asked to decide whether the slaves should be freed and sent back to their African homeland or returned to the Spanish colony of Cuba, where they would be cruelly executed. Although both the Spanish and U.S. governments wanted Judson to send the runaways back to Cuba, Judson ordered the blacks to be freed and returned to Africa. The case, known as the *Amistad* case, became famous because it marked one of the first occasions on which blacks succeeded in using the U.S. legal system to fight for justice. Judson died in 1853, before the outbreak of the Civil War. The story of the *Amistad* captives has been told in several books and in *Amistad,* a film directed by Steven Spielberg.

Samuel May: After Prudence Crandall's school closed, May spent a month traveling around New England, urging Americans to abolish slavery and discussing the fate of the school. In 1834 he left Brooklyn and became director of a college for teachers. He also became a conductor on the Underground Railroad and helped slaves from Virginia, Kentucky, Tennessee, and Louisiana reach freedom. Although he hated violence, May supported the Civil War because he felt it was the only way to end slavery. In later years he fought for coed schools. He campaigned vigorously for women's rights and was one of the first clergymen to support giving women the right to vote. He never forgot Prudence. He kept her portrait with him until his death in 1871, and bequeathed it to Cornell University, where it now hangs, on the condition that the university agree to accept women into its classes. May was also the uncle of Louisa May Alcott, the famous author of *Little Women*.

Arthur Tappan: He continued to fight for abolitionist causes. He became president of the American and Foreign Anti-Slavery Society and helped support the Underground Railroad. His business failed in 1842, but by the early 1850s he was able to retire and devote all his time to good works. He died in July 1865.

Notes

A Note on Sources

TRYING TO FIND OUT ABOUT the life of a little-known historical figure like Prudence Crandall is, to say the least, challenging. Modern studies of her life are few. No complete collection of Prudence's papers exists. Some documents are unpublished; relevant materials are scattered throughout numerous collections across the country; and some materials are too rare to be allowed out on interlibrary loan. I have, however, been fortunate to have access to the UCLA Research Library, which provided me with to many published primary sources. I am also deeply grateful to librarians at the Kansas State Historical Society, the Connecticut State Library, and the New-York Historical Society who located, copied, and sent me many materials from their collections. Susan Strane's thoroughly researched *A Whole-Souled Woman* has been a valuable source, and Marvis Olive Welch's *Prudence Crandall: A Biography* has been particularly useful because it reprints many primary documents—particularly letters—to which I would not otherwise have had access.

1. "A Little More Learning"

"barbecued": Strane, p. 21.

Mariah: Some modern books call her Marcia. Strane, however, believes that this is due to a misreading of one of Prudence's letters and notes (p. 233, note 13), that the name appears as Mariah or Maria in other contemporary documents. I have followed Strane's usage.

"feelings...awaken": Prudence's description of her feelings comes from an article she published in the *Liberator* on May 25, 1833.

"Miss Crandall . . . I want to get a little . . . learning": The conversation between Prudence and Sarah was recorded in the *Liberator* on May 25, 1833.

"a curse and a contagion": Abdy, p. 122. The professor, Edward Abdy, who traveled to the United States in the 1830s, indignantly described the kind of treatment free blacks received in the North. He noted, for example, that a free black could not get a license to run a tavern in New York.

2. "The School May Sink"

"nigger girl": May, p. 41.

"destructive to the best interests": quotation from a resolution passed by the mayor and city council of New Haven, Connecticut, quoted in Von Holst, p. 98.

"sink . . . I will not give up": This quotation comes from the *Moline Republican,* February 7,1890. This meeting is also reported with slight variations in the *Topeka Daily Capital* on April 4, 1886; Larned, p. 491; and Strane, p. 27. Strane calls this woman Mrs. Peters. Larned and the *Republican* do not give her a name, and the *Daily Capital* refers to her as Mrs. White. I have followed the *Daily Capital* usage.

might not be able to repay: In a letter to the Reverend Jocelyn on April 17, 1833 (see Springarn, p. 82), Prudence said she had enough money to pay her debts, but given the expense of keeping up a big house and the amount she was likely to be able to earn as a teacher, she would probably have had to sell the house she used as a school.

American Colonization Society . . . send . . . black Americans . . . back to Africa: This idea was still being discussed in 1858 when soon-to-be president Abraham Lincoln debated his political rival Stephen Douglas. Lincoln said that although his impulse was to send African Americans back to their native land, he felt the idea was impractical and that blacks used to life in the United States would rapidly die in Africa. He also noted that there were not enough funds or ships to take all American blacks back to their original home.

white girls . . . didn't seem . . . upset: May, p. 41.

"very obstinate girl": from a statement made by Prudence's brother Reuben, quoted in Strane, p. 9. Strane says this is taken from "Canterbury Pilgrims," an unpublished manuscript by Rena Clisby, to which I have not had access. Reuben, incidentally, appears to have been the only member of the Crandall family who seriously disapproved of Prudence's school for black women.

"Mr. Garrison, I am": Prudence's letter of January 18, 1833, to William Lloyd Garrison is quoted in Garrison, vol. 1, pp. 315–16.

3. "Six Scholars"

"Mr. Garrison: the lady who wrote": Prudence's note dated January 29, 1833, to William Lloyd Garrison, quoted in Garrison, vol. 1, p. 316.

"madman": May, p. 33.

"fanatic": ibid.

"murderers . . . robbers": from statements made by William Lloyd Garrison when writing for an antislavery newspaper in Baltimore, quoted in Merrill, *Against Wind and Tide,* p. 31.

twenty-five . . . subscribers . . . were white: letter from William Lloyd Garrison to Simeon Jocelyn on May 30,1831, in Springarn, p. 79.

"keep more cool . . . on fire": May, pp. 36–37.

one out of every twenty: Bennett, p. 295.

"positions of responsibility": Adler, p. 52, quoting from a plan for a black school in the "Proceedings of the National Colored Convention held in Rochester, July 6, 7 and 8, 1853."

"greatest place": Washington, p. 42.

"I shall . . . obtain six scholars": letter from Prudence to William Lloyd Garrison on February 12, 1833, quoted in Garrison, vol. 1, pp. 316–17.

"praiseworthy": Prudence's conversation with Mr. Packer is described in a letter from Prudence to William Lloyd Garrison written on February 12, 1833, in Garrison, vol. 1, p. 317.

"peace and quietness": *Kansas City Journal,* March 28, 1886.

4. "Moses Had a Black Wife"

"most powerful men": quoting a letter from Prudence to Simeon Jocelyn dated February 26, 1833, in Springarn, p. 81.

"do everything . . . to destroy": ibid. The dates of these events are confusing. Prudence's letter indicates that the meeting occurred on the 26th; Strane says it occurred on the 25th.

"Mr. Jocelyn, Sir": ibid.

"Moses had a black wife": Larned, p. 492. I have paraphrased Frost's words based on descriptions of this meeting in Larned and Strane, pp. 35–36.

5. "*Will Not You. . . Be My Attorney?*"

"richly deserved," "pleasant": *Liberator,* May 2, 1833.

"that wrong-headed": conversation between May and his father, reported in May, p. 28.

"Although I am a stranger to you": letter from Samuel May to Prudence Crandall dated February 27, 1833, quoted in Welch, p. 40.

"combatant": Catherine Beecher, quoted in Strane, p. 39. Catherine Beecher was the sister of Harriet Beecher Stowe, whose famous novel, *Uncle Tom's Cabin,* helped arouse antislavery sentiment before the Civil War.

"Will you . . . be my attorney?": The conversation between Prudence and May is quoted in May, p. 43. May's abolitionist friend George Benson accompanied him on his first trip to Prudence's house. Since Benson's role is not central to the story and accounts of the part he played at that meeting and at the subsequent town meeting differ, I have chosen not to discuss his participation in the text.

6. "*Men of Canterbury. . . . Hear Me!*"

"persons, property and reputations": All quotations from proceedings of the town meeting come from the *Liberator*, March 16, 1833; May, pp. 44–46, and Larned, pp. 493–94.

"Heathenism Outdone": *Liberator,* March 16, 1833.

"nigger school": All quotations from the meeting between May and Judson have been taken from May, pp. 46–50.

"In the midst of this affliction": letter from Prudence to Simeon Jocelyn dated April 17, 1833, quoted in Springarn, p. 83.

7. "Miss Crandall Has Commenced Her School"

"We have received": *Liberator*, April 27, 1833.

"whipped on the naked body": Larned, p. 495, quoting the writ served on Prudence and Ann Eliza.

female schoolteacher's monthly salary: Foner and Pacheco note (p. xi) that in 1847 a female schoolteacher in Connecticut was paid $6.50 per month.

"land if not . . . civilized world": May, p. 51, relates that he spoke to Ann Eliza Hammond (whom he calls Eliza Ann). Strane, p. 70, states that this incident occurred after a similar warrant was served on student Ann Peterson.

"break down the barriers": *Norwich Republican,* quoted in the *Liberator,* April 6, 1833.

"The thought of such opposition": This and all other quotations in this paragraph come from a letter written by Prudence to the Reverend Simeon Jocelyn on April 17, 1833, quoted in Springarn, p. 83.

8. "Unjust . . . and Disgraceful"

"mother . . . abominations": All quotations in this paragraph came from a letter written by Prudence Crandall, originally published in the *Brooklyn Advertiser* and reprinted in the *Liberator* on May 25, 1833.

"My family . . . setters up": Strane, p. 34, from "Canterbury Pilgrims," an unpublished manuscript by Rena Clisby to which I have not had access.

"destroy any of the rights": All quotations from Pardon Crandall's letter come from the *Kansas City Journal,* March 28, 1886.

"No person . . . shall": May, p. 52.

"unjust": Welch, p. 61, quoting the *Emancipator,* June 22, 1833.

"If you go to your daughter's": This conversation is reported in the *Topeka Daily Capital,* April 4, 1886.

"calm and resolute": May, p. 50.

"weary, weary": *Kansas City Journal,* March 28, 1886.

9. "SAVAGE BARBARITY!"

"how bad . . . wicked": May, p. 56.

"colored persons": Welch, p. 69, quoting the arrest warrant.

"Not guilty": The conversation between Prudence and Rufus Adams is quoted in ibid.

"was in the hands of": The conversation between May and the messenger is quoted in May, p. 53.

"If . . . you hestitate": The conversation between May and Prudence is quoted in May, p. 55.

"SAVAGE BARBARITY": *Liberator,* July 6, 1833.

"FEMALES INTO PRISON": *Female Advocate,* reprinted in the *Liberator* on August 17, 1833.

"In prison for teaching": Yacovone, p. 50.

"[Miss Crandall] has stepped out": *Windham County Advertiser,* reprinted in the *Liberator,* July 20, 1833.

New York Commercial Advertiser: The passsage criticizing Prudence is quoted in Strane, p. 84.

"Priscilla": Strane, p. 84.

10. Under Attack

"occupied by white females": Abdy, p. 201.

"For my part": Abdy, p. 195.

11. Miss Crandall on Trial

The presiding judge: The case was actually heard by a panel of three judges; however, only the presiding judge, Joseph Eaton, seems to have played a major part in the proceedings.

one juror: Strane, p. 97, notes that one juror who had signed the petition requesting passage of the Black Law was excused, but another who voted for the law was allowed to serve on the jury.

"kept a school": The exchanges between Welch and the witnesses are quoted in Fuller, pp. 77–78. The rest of the account is drawn from May, pp. 66–69; *Liberator,* August 31, 1833; Abdy, p. 205; Foner and Pacheco, pp. 28–29; Welch, pp. 80–82; and Strane, pp. 97–103.

12. More Trouble

"not to indulge in angry feelings": All quotations in this paragraph come from "An address written by one of Miss Crandall's scholars," published in the *Liberator,* August 3, 1833.

"You need not send": *Liberator*, November 2, 1833. The *Liberator* does not mention the doctor's name. May, p. 59, says it was "the physician of the village," who, at this time, was Dr. Harris.

"degraded caste": Fuller, p. 83, quoting Judge Daggett's charge to the jury. Interested readers will find extensive quotes from the legal proceeding in Prudence's cases in Fuller's book.

13. Fire!

"What does this mean?": from a partial transcription of Frederick Olney's trial in the *Unionist,* March 13, 1834.

"feloniously, voluntarily": ibid.

14. "The Choicest Blessing"

"unusually handsome": This phrase appears in a letter from Helen Benson to William Lloyd Garrison written on April 3, 1834, quoted in Strane, p. 138.

"I wish I had a lover": poem written by Prudence Crandall, quoted in Welch, pp. 192–93. It is difficult to determine the date of this poem. Welch implies that it was found in a scrapbook dating from the 1880s; however, on p. 191, Welch also indicates that at least some material in this book comes from "The Windham County Transcript," which suggests that the poem might have been written while Prudence was still living in Connecticut.

"choicest blessing": letter from Helen Benson to William Lloyd Garrison dated June 9, 1834, quoted in Welch, p. 101.

"to Miss Crandall": Welch, p. 97.

"praiseworthy and heroic conduct": *Liberator,* September 13, 1843.

"If Miss Crandall": *Boston Press*, quoted in the *Liberator,* August 3, 1833.

"private school" "evening school": *Liberator,* February 1, 1834.

"very disagreeable": Helen Benson to William Lloyd Garrison on June 2, 1834, in Welch, p. 100.

"almost perfect being": Helen Benson to William Lloyd Garrison on June 16, 1834, quoted in Strane, p. 137.

"could make Prudence believe": Helen Benson to William Lloyd Garrison on June 9, 1834, quoted in Welch, p. 101.

"America belongs to a race": Welch, p. 229, reprinting Judson's argument before the Supreme Court of Errors.

"much happiness": William Lloyd Garrison to Helen Benson on August 18, 1834, in Merrill, *Letters of William Lloyd Garrison,* p. 399.

15. "For Sale"

"almost blistered": May, p. 71.

"I felt ashamed": ibid.

"place of communion": Welch, pp. 107–8, quoting an essay by "one of Miss Crandall's juvenile pupils."

"For sale": *Liberator,* September 20, 1834.

Chapter 16: "Deep Convictions of Right"

"I am glad": The dialogue and details of the encounter come from Thayer, p. 211.

"old squash-head": Strane, p. 198.

"I am earnestly engaged": *Topeka Daily Capital,* October 18, 1885.

"weep tears of blood": All quotations from Philip Pearl come from a letter from Theodore Weld to Lewis Tappan, written June 8, 1837, quoted in Barnes, p. 397.

"Our heroine": Anonymous, *Connecticut Magazine,* July 1899.

"She was right": *Springfield (Mass.) Republican,* quoted in the *Topeka Daily Capital,* April 4, 1886.

"I do not consider": *Topeka Daily Capital,* April 4, 1886.

"If the people of Connecticut": Thayer, p. 214.

"Mind has great power": *Moline Republican,* February 7, 1890.

"Preach the truth": ibid.

"She had deep convictions": ibid.

Epilogue

"The Negro baby": Bennett, pp. 387–88.

Bibliography

Abdy, Edward S. *Journal of a Residence and Tour in the United States of North America from April, 1833 to October, 1834*. Vol. 1. New York: Negro Universities Press (division of Greenwood Publishing), 1969.

Adams, Mildred. "Rampant Women." In *Victory: How Women Won It: A Centennial Symposium 1840–1940 by the National American Woman Suffrage Association*. New York: H. W. Wilson, 1940.

Adler, Mortimer J., Charles Van Doren, and George Ducas, eds. *The Negro in American History*. Vol. 3, "Slaves and Masters 1564–1854." Chicago: Encyclopedia Britannica Educational Corp., 1969.

Anonymous. "Andrew Thompson Judson," a pamphlet produced by the Prudence Crandall Museum, Canterbury, Conn., n.d.

Anonymous. Department of Education Press Release, October 14, 2003: "Paige Cites Progress in Black Education but Notes Achievement Gap Has Widened over Past Two Decades." Published by the U.S. Department of State International Information Program (usinfo.state.gov/usa/blackhis/pr101403htm), based on "Status and Trends in the Education of Blacks," released by the National Center for Education Statistics.

Anonymous. "Prudence Crandall." *Connecticut Magazine* 5, no. 7 (July 1899): 386–88.

Anonymous. "Students of Prudence Crandall 1833–1834," a pamphlet produced by the Prudence Crandall Museum, Canterbury, Conn., n.d.

Barber, John Warner. *Connecticut Historical Collections: Containing a general collection of interesting facts, traditions, biographical sketches, anecdotes, etc. relating to the History and Antiquities of every town in Connecticut with geographical descriptions*. New Haven: Durrie & Peck, 1838.

Barnes, Gilbert, and Dwight L. Dumond. *Letters of Theodore Dwight Weld, Angelina Grimké Weld, and Sarah Grimké 1822–1844*. Vol 1. D. Appleton-Century, 1934.

Baush, Norma. *Framing American Divorce: From the Revolutionary Generation to the Victorians*. Berkeley: University of California Press, 1999. (ark.cdlib.org/ark:/13030/ft10000347/)

Bennett, Lerone, Jr. *Before the Mayflower: A History of Black America*. 5th ed. New York: Penguin, 1982.

Blum, John, et al., eds. *The National Experience: A History of the United States*. 6th ed. San Diego: Harcourt, Brace, Jovanovich, 1985.

Brown, William Wells. *The Negro in the American Rebellion: His Heroism and His Fidelity*. 1867. Making of America Web site: www.hti.umich.edu/m/moagrp.

Canfield, James H. "Prudence Crandall: The Continuation of the Story of an Interesting Life." *Topeka Daily Capital,* October 18, 1885, p. 5.

Cohen, Adam. "The Supreme Struggle." *New York Times,* January 18, 2004, section 4A, pp. 22–24, 38.

Foner, Philip S. *History of Black Americans*. Vol. 2, *From the Emergence of the Cotton Kingdom to the Eve of the Compromise of 1850.* Contributions in American History 102. Westport, Conn.: Greenwood Press, 1983.

Foner, Philip S., and Josephine F. Pacheco. *Three Who Dared: Prudence Crandall, Margaret Douglas, Myrtilla Miner—Champions of Antebellum Black Education.* Contributions in Women's Studies 47. Westport, Conn.: Greenwood Press, 1984.

Fredrickson, George M. *The Black Image in the White Mind: The Debate on Afro-American Character and Destiny 1817–1914*. New York: Harper & Row, 1971.

Fuller, Edmund. *Prudence Crandall: An Incident of Racism in Nineteenth-Century Connecticut*. Middletown, Conn.: Wesleyan University Press, 1971.

Garrison, Wendell Phillips, and Francis Jackson Garrison. *William Lloyd Garrison, 1805–1879: The Story of His Life Told by His Children*. New York: The Century Co., 1885–89.

Greeley, Horace. *The American Conflict: A History of the Great Rebellion in the United States of America 1860–64: Its Causes, Incidents and Results, 1865–66.* Making of America Web site: www.hti.umich.edu/m/moagrp.

Hughes, Langston, Milton Meltzer, and C. Eric Lincoln. *A Pictorial History of Blackamericans*. New York: Crown, 1983.

Jackson, Kenneth T., ed. *The Encyclopedia of New York City*. New Haven: Yale University Press, 1995.

Jones, Howard. *Mutiny on the* Amistad*: The Saga of a Slave Revolt and Its Impact on American Abolition, Law, and Diplomacy*. New York: Oxford University Press, 1987.

Larned, Ellen D. *History of Windham County Connecticut*. Vol. 2, *1760–1880*. Worcester, Mass.: Charles Hamilton, 1880.

Mattingly, Carol. *Appropriate[ing] Dress: Women's Rhetorical Style in Nineteenth-Century America*. Carbondale, Ill.: Southern Illinois University Press, 2002.

May, Samuel J. *Some Recollections of Our Antislavery Conflict*. Boston: Fields, Osgood & Co., 1869.

McCarron, Anna T. "The Trial of Prudence Crandall for [sic] Crime of Educating Negroes in Connecticut." *Connecticut Magazine* 12, no. 2 (2nd quarter, 1908): 225–32.

Merrill, Walter M. *Against Wind and Tide: A Biography of Wm.* [sic] *Lloyd Garrison*. Cambridge: Harvard University Press, 1963.

———. *The Letters of William Lloyd Garrison*. Vol. 1, *I Will Be Heard 1822–1835*. Cambridge: Belknap Press of Harvard University Press, 1971.

Meyer, Ruth. "School Integration Pioneer Buried in Kansas." *Wichita Morning Eagle,* December 6, 1956.

Morrisson, Mary Foulke. "That Word Male." In *Victory: How Women Won It: A Centennial Symposium 1840–1940,* by the National American Woman Suffrage Association. New York: H. W. Wilson, 1940.

Mumford, Thomas James. *Memoir of Samuel Joseph May,* 1873. Making of America Web site: www.hti.umich.edu/m/moagrp.

Nashold, Jessica. "The Final Years of Prudence Crandall's Life." *Mendota Reporter,* April 29, 1981.

Randall, Laura (interviewer). "When Schools Were Shacks." *New York Times,* January 18, 2004, section 4A, p. 27.

Rozar, Lily B. "Black Law Pointed at Her." *Independence Reporter,* April 14, 1957.

Selby, Paul. *Anecdotal Lincoln: Speeches, Stories and Yarns of the 'Immortal Abe.'* Chicago: Thompson and Thomas, 1900.

Springarn, Arthur B. "Abolition Letters Collected by Captain Arthur B. Springarn." *Journal of Negro History* 18, no. 1 (January 1933): 78–84.

Stanton, Elizabeth Cady, Susan B. Anthony, and Matilda J. Gage, eds. *History of Woman Suffrage.* Vol. 3, *1876–1885*. Salem, N.H: Ayer, 1985.

Strane, Susan. *A Whole-Souled Woman: Prudence Crandall and the Education of Black Women*. New York: W. W. Norton, 1990.

Strother, Horatio T. *The Underground Railroad in Connecticut*. Middletown, Conn.: Wesleyan University Press, 1962.

Thayer, George B. *Pedal and Path: Across the Continent Awheel and Afoot*. Hartford, Conn.: Case, Lockwood & Brainard, n.d.

Von Holst, H. [Herman]. *The Constitutional and Political History of the United States, 1876–92*. Making of America Web site: www.hti.umich.edu/m/moagrp.

Washington, Booker T. *Up from Slavery: An Autobiography*. Boston: Houghton Mifflin, 1928.

Welch, Marvis Olive. *Prudence Crandall: A Biography*. Manchester, Conn.: Jason Publishers, 1983.

Wexler, Stanford. *The Civil Rights Movement: An Eyewitness History*. New York: Facts on File, 1993.

Yacovone, Donald. *Samuel Joseph May and the Dilemmas of the Liberal Persuasion 1797–1871*. Philadelphia: Temple University Press, 1991.

Newspapers

Kansas City Journal (Kansas State Historical Society).

Liberator. Microfilm. Ann Arbor, Mich. University Microfilms, 1956.

Moline (Kansas) Republican (Kansas State Historical Society).

Topeka Daily Capital (Kansas State Historical Society).

Unionist (New-York Historical Society).

Index

Frontispiece, back of jacket, pp. 1, 99: Prudence Crandall, portrait by Francis Alexander, Division of Rare and Manuscript Collections, Cornell University Library.

pp. 2, 10, 15, 26, 59, 61, 69, 81, 85, 87, 89: David E. Tripp.

pp. 3, 97: Getty Images.

p. 4: General Research Division, The New York Public Library, Astor, Lenox and Tilden Foundations.

pp. 8, 12, 30, 36, 39, 55, 56, 107, 115: Collection of the Prudence Crandall Museum, State of Connecticut. Note: Photos of individuals have been altered slightly to fit oval format. Images have been printed with colored ink over a background color.

p. 18: From a daguerreotype by T. B. Shaw, P. S. Duval, Lith.: Philadelphia. On stone by Albert Newsam. Sophia Smith Collection, Smith College. Note: Photo has been altered slightly to fit oval format. Image has been printed with colored ink over a background color.

p. 33: Frontispiece from *Memoir of Samuel Joseph May* (Boston: Roberts Bros., 1873). Rare E449.M467. Division of Rare and Manuscript Collections, Cornell University Library.

p. 46: Library of Congress, Photoduplication Service.

p. 49: Stack's Rare Coins, New York City.

p. 71: The Amistad Research Center at Tulane University, New Orleans, Louisiana. Note: Shape of photo has been altered to fit oval format. Image has been printed with colored ink over a background color.

p. 92: Photograph by Warren's Portraits, 465 Washington St., Boston, Mass. Sophia Smith Collection, Smith College. Note: Image has been printed with colored ink over a background color.

p. 94: Library of Congress, Prints and Photographs Division, LC-USZ62-11766.

p. 105: Library of Congress, Prints and Photographs Division, LC-USZ62-22396.

p. 106: Connecticut State Library, caged collection. C. R. Lang Photography.

p. 108: Kansas State Historical Society, Topeka, Kansas. Note: Image has been printed with colored ink over a background color.

p. 112: Author's collection.

p. 117: Hank Walker/Time Life Pictures/Getty Images.

p. 118: Courtesy of the *Arkansas Democrat-Gazette.*

p. 119: Paul Slade/Hulton Archive/Getty Images.

p. 120: Steve Liss/Time Life Pictures/Getty Images.